THE LIFE
Memoirs of the Hood Conservative

Cecilia S. Johnson

Copyright 2020, Cecilia S Johnson

All rights reserved. This book or any portion thereof may not be reproduced or used in any manner whatsoever without the expressed written consent of the Publisher and/or Author except for the use of brief quotations in a book review or relative source. Any plagiarism committed without proper reference and acknowledgement of this book and/or Author is illegal and considered eligible for lawsuit.

Printed in the United States of America

-Cecilia S. Johnson-

<u>Introduction</u>

When I first decided to make this work, I initially thought I was going to write a full-blown political book. The thought to include so much of my personal life and my personal testimony never really crossed my mind. After being convinced by my friend that if I was going to write a true memoir that I must include the true essence of Cecilia, I did just that. I am glad she talked me into it. As I went into my writing process, I thought of how many people I would be able to help with my story. A lot of things that I talked about in this book I have not thought about in what seems like forever. A lot of this required me to dig deep and revisit experiences in dark rooms that I never plan to be in again. A lot of it required me to open wounds that have healed just so that I can recall the story.

I did not realize how emotional this process would be for me. I looked at it as a fun undertaking at first. And it was. But it was also one filled with many tears. Many feelings of sickness. Mostly, it required me to visit "*CiCi.*" CiCi is the child version of Cecilia. CiCi was the part of me that desired to have a lot of fun. There were a lot of good times with her but there also comes a lot of pain. I did not know that I would have to dig so deep in the corners of my soul just to get the story out. As nervous and anxious as I am for this book to be read by someone's eyes other than my own, I cannot help but to feel proud.

I really did this. I really told my story. I suspect that a lot of people will be shocked after reading my story and a lot of people will get more than what I bargained for from this book. For a lot of you, this is your introduction to me. Whether you like what I have to say is indifferent to me. What matters is that you have a full understanding of who I am. Did you really walk away from this book feeling as if you gave an honest peek into this soul of mine? With all the things that I wanted to write about, I thought this book was going to be way bigger than it is. I am surprised to see what my number count is as I finish writing it.

As you embark on the journey that is my life, I hope that you can accept and respect the gift that I give you in the form of my transparency. I will be honest in

saying that transparency was a bit difficult at times. But I felt my life by book would not be complete without it. God really gave me the courage to be forthcoming about who I am. And I thank him for that.
Inside this book you will find the raw and unedited story of my life. You will find pain, happiness, joy, and turmoil. But what you will not find is fear. I don't live my life by it, and I didn't write with it. I completely allowed myself to be free and let myself go without second-guessing my decision to write my story nor without second-guessing the words on the paper. I never thought I would write a book. Yet after writing this one I look forward to our next experience together with me as an Author and you as the reader.
    I am many things to many people, and I am even more to myself. I hold myself in extremely high regard. I expect a lot out of myself if I say too much. This book is a testament to that. So, I will not hold you up any longer as you have a book to read!   -*Cecilia S. Johnson*

Great-Great Grandmother & Father | May Francis Twiggs & Zeke Keith

Chapter 1

Like most people, a lot of who I am today is heavily influenced by where I'm from and my family. I have had a unique upbringing that allowed me to spend half of my life in an extremely rural area and the other half in an urban jungle. These two places were worlds apart and still *are* in my eyes. While they are very different on the surface, they do have a lot of similarities. The main one being that they are mostly negative, inferior view of the other. Each one criticizes the other based on their choice of environment and living conditions. Nevertheless, they are both an explanation of the person writing these words.

I grew up being a super-aware child. Always in tune with myself and others around me. Maybe this was the reason that from an incredibly young age, I was ever rarely dismissed by the adults in my family from 'grown folks' business'. I could linger around them, picking up on the latest gossip until I grew bored and ran off to play with the other kids' juicy gossip in hand.

I have always been a multi-layered person filled to the brim with life and personality. Remember in the movie "*Shrek*" when he was explaining to Donkey that ogres were like onions? Well, that was me. Not an ogre, although my body grew to be shaped like one, prompting teasing from my peers in my adolescent years. I meant that I am like an onion and I can tell you about every bulb scale, inside and out with the good, the bad, and the dark.

My Mother has always allowed me to be myself and encouraged me to strive to be better tomorrow than I was the day before. Perhaps this is where my love for personal improvement and self-help came from. In my world, there were no limits to what I could do. No was no glass ceiling to try and get in my way and I still to this day believe that. The only thing that could stop me was me and I have always known that to be a choice for me to make. While I would ultimately often get in my own way, I could always shove myself out of the way in order to get things done and move to the next level.

Now, do not misunderstand what I am saying. I'm human just like you and have had to deal with common things such as second guessing myself, beating myself up and the occasional insecurity, but I was always aware of any issue that arose and could quickly overcome them with a few exceptions. My main issue was my weight.

I do not remember a time in my life when I was "*normal-sized.*" My gut had always poked out, love handles stuck to me like glue, and my double chin proved that it was more faithful than the Lord Jesus Christ that had died on the cross for my sins. As a child, kids didn't really tease me about it mainly because I was somewhat of a bully and was always down to throw hands if you got on my nerves. Hence the reason I was always allowed to be the Pink Ranger whenever we played Power Rangers.

All my teasing came from my family members. I come from a very tough family that in many ways sharpened me for the real world. My skin was made thicker than an elephant's, thanks to our roasting sessions. Our favorite hobby is sitting around roasting each other for all our shortcomings, mishaps, and any downright dumb things we had said. It is our unique way of bonding and showing love.

Jokes aside, we are a close family. You mess with one of us, you mess with all of us. I am sure a lot of families are like this, but a lot of families are fortunate enough to be the "Johnsons." I guess from the outside looking in, my family probably does not seem like anything special, but we are. Filled with so much personality and talent, our only sin seemed to be our ability to turn that talent into the fortunes that I knew we were capable of. Everyone has their strengths and knows how to play to them, but my Mama is the most special of the bunch.

One of the truly sweetest people to ever walk the Earth, she always had an aura about her that seemed to draw people in as if she were casting a spell. If there was ever such a thing as a good witch, it was my Mother. Her smile would light up every room she enters and was as contagious as any disease. She was always eager to jump to someone's assistance and most times would put their needs before her own- A trait I would grow to dislike in her. Instead of focusing on herself, her heart was always easily distracted by what someone else needed. A giving person, she never asked anything in return. To this day, I am often charged with *"acting just like yo' Mama"*. I take it as a compliment.

A tomboy who wears her heart on her sleeve, she was always immensely popular. Even though I obviously was not there, I have heard the stories. A good student, star of the basketball team, and a leader in her class, she was known for all the right reasons. It is rare that the popular girl would give you the shirt off her back but that was Emma and still is.

At the ripe age of 14, she met and was approached by one of her oldest brother's best friend, Will. Tall, dark, and handsome, he lived a few towns over and liked what he saw. His insecurities and immaturity would ultimately end their relationship but would birth one of the greatest gifts this world has seen, Cecilia S. Johnson.

Over the next two years, they snuck around and dated against my grandfather's approval. Although it was hard for her to see it, my Mother was *Paw-Paw's* favorite. What his approach lacked in affection it had made up for it in tough love. While he displayed tough love to all of his kids, one clearly stood out from the rest. Grandpa was a no nonsense, reserved man. He was a farmer who raised chickens and hogs with the help of his children. My Mother and her siblings spent a great portion of their childhood and teen years tending to and slaughtering hogs. Thank GOD they were done with by the time I came of age.

My Paw-Paw played no games. At even the slightest sign of disrespect, he would pull out his pistol faster than my Grandma could skin a possum and put it right up to his kids' temple daring them to utter another word. If *"I brought you into this world and I will take you out"* was a person, it was my Grandfather. Given the mindset of our small town, he probably would have gotten away with it. The sheriff would have considered it a closed case after he explained that his child had committed the highly offensive crime of back-talk.

We hail from a small town tucked away in the Southeast corner of Arkansas called Lake Village. Resting on the center of the largest oxbow lake in North America, Lake Chicot, our personalities seemed too big for the small town with a population of 2,500. Yet, there we were. As the years passed, we slowly began to migrate to Kansas City for more opportunity and a better life, even if it was against my will.

My Mother and Father continued their secret relationship even after an encounter with my Grandpa's rifle that almost proved fatal for them both. Yes, my Grandpa was strapped and yes, it runs in the blood.

My Mother, wanting to spend quality time with my Father lied to my Grandmother about staying over a friend's house, she of course got caught. As my father was bringing her home, he proceeded to hoist her up so she could climb into the window and sneak into her room because she had left her key. Paw-Paw allowed them to almost accomplish this before revealing himself on the porch and cocking his rifle. BOOM! He shot the first shot at my Father, missing him by a few inches. BOOM! The second one was for my Mother.

They dove off the porch and ran for their dear lives because well, that is what you do when you are getting shot at. I must give it to my Mother, she must be something special to have a guy willing to die just to be near her. My Mother returned the next morning where she received the beatdown of a lifetime and the next.

A few months later while she was washing dishes, my Grandpa approached her and told her that she was pregnant. She was confused especially since she had not displayed any symptoms. Two weeks later, there it was, morning sickness.

That was the strange thing about my Grandpa. He was very in tune with women and possessed a man's intuition that was virtually unheard of. Being raised with mostly sisters, he was afforded the chance to witness them up close and personal.

After learning of her new situation, my Mother noticed my Father's distance. It was a distance that would only grow wider the bigger her belly got. Alone and unwed, she felt ashamed even though by her accounts no one ever shamed her for her situation. No one treated her any different for her obvious sins, yet she felt it. That Halloween, while out Trick-or-Treating, she started to feel painful contractions. After making it home, Paw-Paw informed her that she was in labor and they headed for his station wagon. On the way to the hospital, she could not help but notice how slow he was driving. It seemed like punishment for getting herself in this situation. No matter how much she moaned and groaned in the back seat of his car, he did not speed up. Once they arrived at the hospital, my Mother's doctor greeted them. He was one of the best doctors in the Delta; Perhaps, this was due to him possessing the same intuition that my Grandfather did. The doctor had birthed damn near all of Chicot County until he quit and moved to Little Rock and became an abortionist. While there's a lot of money in bringing life into this world, there's even more in ending it.

On November 1, 1987, I came barging into the world. Loud, proud, and weighing almost 10 pounds, I was adorable if I might say so myself. Usually a hard-ass, my Grandpa had found his soft spot. I wish I could say the same for my Father.

He stopped by that night while on break but quickly left. He was driving a pickup making deliveries and had to get back to work. He saw me once more before announcing he was moving to Dallas for better opportunities. Before he left, my Mother discovered that he had another little girl, less than a year older than me in Greenville, Mississippi, right across the Mississippi bridge. She was devastated but like me, you cannot keep my Mother down for long. Before you knew it, she was up and running. Even with a baby on her hip, she seemed to not skip a beat. Jumping right back into school, everyone was obsessed with her bubbly new accessory. And why wouldn't they be?

She was never short of a babysitter and could continue to enjoy her teenage years. Less than two years later, she had done it again. This time with a married farmer twice her age. He was a close friend with my Grandfather. Strangely enough, he accurately approved of this relationship. In September of 1989, she gave birth to her second child, a boy named Trevor. We were complete opposites. Where he was quiet and more reserved, I was loud and demanding of attention. Clearly, not much has changed in my life. Shortly after discovering she was pregnant with her third child five months later, she had a larger problem on her hands.

One afternoon, my Mother noticed Trevor being unusually fussy. After picking him up, she felt his hot body temperature and immediately rushed him to the hospital. My brother had been diagnosed with spinal meningitis and was abruptly put on life support. Day after day, she sat with him in the hospital. After two weeks of no improvement, she made the hardest decision she had to make, and she decided to take him off of life support. He was in a vegetative state and there was nothing the doctors could do to save him. That July, she buried him without even enough for a headstone in our family plot. It was not until I typed those words that I realized that I would be put in the same situation almost 25 years later to the day.

Despite her traumatic situation, she continued to hold her head up high. This is the point of the story where most would have given up, stopped living, and withdrew into their shell and stayed there until it was safe to come out. But She didn't.

In October, she gave birth to her third child, a beautiful, chunky baby named Jalissa. After a few years, my Mother noticed that Jalissa was a little behind in terms of development and my Mother had her tested. The results were yet another blow to my prize fighter of a Mother. Due to unknown reasons, my little sister had a learning disability. She would ultimately be diagnosed with Mental Retardation but perhaps the most admirable thing about her is that she does not see herself as such. Yes, she acknowledges that she is a little different, but she never really shied away from being herself.

From a young age, like most first born children, it was my job to care for and protect my baby sister- Even if she did not understand or appreciate it all the time. My Mother worked a lot so most of the time we were left to entertain ourselves and boy did we. We had huge imaginations and rarely needed toys to have a great time. Maybe that is why we never really had many toys. We could make up entire movies and would act them out for hours until completion. More reserved and shy, when we were alone, I would often let her be the star of the show or select what we would be doing that day.

Even as a young child, I could always sense what people needed or secretly desired and would do what I could to help them fulfill that fantasy, even if it was behind closed doors. As I have gotten older, that trait has developed into me always wanting to help people do whatever their heart desired. Sometimes it is trying out for the team, auditioning for that play, singing in the talent show, or starting a business. I have somehow always known the words to say or ways to make them feel at ease, confident, and as if they could conquer the world. I think this is a gift that my sister gave me or at least showed me that I possessed it. For as mean as I can be at times, I love being able to encourage and inspire others. I get such a high from having someone come to me with sunken shoulders and leave with an erect back and huge smile on their face.

As Jalissa got older, our relationship became more negative. My dominant personality and desire for her to be her best was controlling and domineering while her often motionless attitude and lack of thankfulness was seen as disrespectful and ungratefulness. Jalissa has the kind of disability where she doesn't appear to be anything other than a normal person yet there will usually come a time where she would say something that was would encourage a state of confusion by people and would often lead to them saying something to the tune of "*Are you retarded or something?*" with a chuckle. This hurt me more than it did her. I did not like the idea of people misunderstanding her or making her feel uncomfortable about something she had no control over. To prevent this, I would start having conversations with people before they met her, and things changed. Instead of them treating her differently, they embraced her more and if she ever said anything crazy or off topic, they would just laugh and tell her how funny she was. My friends would always be ok and happy even to have her join us and hang around us.

As I write this, tears are rolling down my cheeks. Perhaps it is due to how far we have come in our relationship. We have VASTLY different personalities that have clashed a lot in the past, but I am happy to report that we are in a much better place. We understand each other a lot more and act accordingly. My Mother has enjoyed this perhaps more than we care to hear about. She, like me, appreciated unity.

Like a lot of single parent households, we moved around a lot. For a year of my childhood, we lived with our cousin in Memphis, Tennessee. She and my Mother were very close, but my sister and I saw her as mean with very aggressively expressive eyebrows that resulted in us hardly ever leaving our room. One top of this, she had a dog and Jalissa and I were not exactly animal people unless we had a hand in raising it. He was a golden retriever and I know what you are thinking.

"Golden retrievers are amazing!"
"They make the best family dogs!"
"They're so nice and sweet!"

(Major eye roll)

This dog was the damn devil! It growled at us every chance we got, leaving us paralyzed with fear. We were oftentimes afraid to even go to the bathroom and this proved to be for a good reason. One day, the "sweet family dog" chased Jalissa around the apartment and bit her pinky toe when she fell, and it was sheer terror. I cried more than she did because I wasn't fast enough to protect her. Instead of putting the dog down, our cousin kept him and even defended the monster. It is at this point I discovered my annoyance for dog-lovers. How could you put an animal above human comfort and safety? *How* is my middle name after this person?

My hatred for dogs was not the only thing that came from my stent in Memphis. It was that I developed the most disgusting habit that I have yet to kick to this day. To a small-town girl like myself, Memphis was an even bigger town. This is my first time being around people that did not know my greatness so what did I do? I made myself smaller- Not in size but in personality.

I was a fish out of water. Despite this, the most popular group of girls recruited me to be their friend my first week there. They were all pretty and I liked being around the pretty girls. It made me feel more pretty, as if their beauty could rub off on an ugly duckling like myself. This was also my first time being a follower. The leader of the pact often determined what we were, what we liked to do, and even who we were but I did not argue. I think I also kind of liked being able to not be in the forefront all the time, something that was often forced on me back home.

One beautiful day as we were walking home, a new order came from our boss. *"So, I was thinking the other night that we have nothing to set us apart from the other girls at school. We do not look any different. So, I think we should start biting our nails. It's so cool and different!"* We had all agreed to the suggestion. Whenever she had a 'thought', that was code for this is the way it is from now on. So, we did as she said and started biting our nails. It was so weird at first, but I got used to it. We all did.

A few months later, we returned home, and my bad habit followed me. No matter what I did, I could not stop it and we tried EVERYTHING. I was determined that this is the price you pay for being a follower and I wanted no parts of it. *I would never be a follower again* I thought in a moment of hopelessness. I guess you can call me a fast learner.

Back home, I felt *at home*. I was a small-town girl at heart. Being one of the most popular kids in school I was always something of a star-even if it was mostly in my head. As an adult now, I realize how fortunate I am to be raised in the kind of environment and place that is Lake Village, Arkansas. A true community, everybody knew everybody. Everybody was your parents' set of eyes and could beat the living daylights out of you, then take you to your parents and hand them the belt or switch and they would proceed to do the same but worse. This time it was personal. Not only did you misbehave but you got caught acting like you didn't have no home training and embarrassed your parents. This is perhaps the only upside of not having a Father in the home, there was only one person to whoop me. Our School Teachers and Principals all also had the authority to spank us. Mr. Watkins, our Principal, even had a thick paddle that looked like the ones kept in frat houses except his was much thicker and I swear he had to be trained by Babe Ruth and Sammy Sosa both on how to swing that thing. Ah, the good old days.

In hindsight, Lake Village was like something from a movie that city folks look down on. Mostly a trailer park area, we even had a club called, you guessed it, *The Trailer*. Everyone of all ages, ethnicities, and financial status went to *The Trailer,* even me. Yes, kids were there too.

Remember in the movie 'Sweet Home Alabama' when Reese Witherspoon returned to her hometown and she chased her husband to the local bar and ran into an old friend? With a surprised look she exclaimed, "You have a baby! In a bar!" Yeah, I saw absolutely nothing odd about that. There are pictures of me floating around somewhere in *The Trailer*. The strong smell of cigarettes surrounding me while my sister and I drank our Sprite and ate our fish. There were even couches for the kids to sleep on when they got tired, but I never did. I spent my night socializing, dancing, and being noisy. I discovered the party animal in me at a young age and loved being *the life of the party*. Since *The Trailer* had no closing hours, the doors did not close until the grown-ups got tired and slowly filtered out of the living ashtray. Speaking of which, my lungs are just now recovering from the smoke.

Lake Village was like most of rural America. You blink and you miss it. A small town with a current population of 2,500 people, it was the perfect place to grow up. I didn't realize it as a child, and I don't think most people who grow up in a slice of Heaven do. Positioned right in the center of Lake Chicot, the largest oxbow lake in North America, it is a true beauty. From a map, Lake Chicot is perfectly shaped in the letter 'C', for 'Cecilia' no doubt. Once a big farm town and huge agricultural area, it has now transitioned into a place where hardly anyone grows their own food and mostly everyone works indoors. It's also a big vacation spot for people from both the east and west coast to relax and escape their busy, demanding lives. My hometown is perfect for that.

Deep down, my rural upbringing has embedded traditional values in me. While my Mother had a unique situation, most of the town were married before having kids. We all collectively went to one of the many churches every Sunday and stayed all day. We did not really mind because the long, drawn out service was usually always followed by a big dinner made by the First Lady of the church and the Deacons' Wives. The dinner was never disappointing. We had fried chicken, greens with ham hocks, sweet corn, pinto beans with neckbones, homemade mac and cheese (it was against the law to serve it from a box at church), green beans, fried catfish and brim, and sweet, buttery cornbread- All of which was served in one sitting.

While my hometown shares a lot of commonalities with most of God's country, it also has many differences. For one, it is slightly mostly black. I assume this is a result of the Chicot County Race Riot of 1871 in which a black Attorney was shot point blank by a white store owner after engaging in an argument with the store owner and two of his friends. The Attorney, Wathal G. Wynn, called the store owner a liar and he killed him. All three white men were immediately arrested for the murder. Wynn, a Republican was accused of trying to recruit other blacks to the party and the three men were Democrats and reportedly members of the Ku Klux Klan. Wynn's brother-in-law was the State Senator and County Judge James W. Mason wrote a letter to an Ohio Republican friend of his about the murder and the alleged KKK ties and it was published in the newspaper which was ultimately published in the *Washington Chronicle* and the *New York Times*. Shortly after, several hundred black men went to the county jail house and broke the three white men out of jail. They took them into the woods and shot them. Black people where I'm from don't play nor do we tolerate any disrespect of any kind.

    What happened next is up for debate depending on what source you are hearing it from. The Democrat press reported that the black community violently reigned terror by destroying the property of the counties whites while Republican media said the Democrats were being dramatic and defended the blacks by saying the reports were exaggerated. Either way, the whites fled the area, leaving mostly by steamboats and most to never return.

In 1873, Mason was arrested for instigating the violence and charged with the murder of the three white men. After several weeks of the trial, he was released on a writ of *habeas corpus* and returned to his position to finish out his term, not bad for a small town.

This leads me to the second biggest difference about my hometown and country, they are mostly Democrats. Since the early 1980's most of our elected officials on the local and state level have been Conservative Democrats despite our history.

Our rich history only adds to our beauty. Rich or poor, black or white, gay or straight, we are there for each other. Growing up in Lake Village has really given me a unique, strong worldview. Our relationships have no barriers. We were raised to respect each other no matter our differences and if you ever *did* try to do that, somebody was always around to beat the black off you.

Cecilia & Jalissa

Chapter 2

In the summer of 1997, I moved back to Lake Village from Camden, Arkansas. Camden was a lot like Lake Village except it was a bit more run down. I had spent the second semester of the 4th grade with my Grandma while my Mother stayed in Lake Village working tirelessly to save money. My sister stayed with her while I was hauled off. Like most things during that time, I did not mind mainly because I understood those kinds of things even as a young child.

My Grandmother was a traditional *Southern Woman*. Church on Sunday followed by Sunday dinner, dresses down to her ankles, white stockings, and a house full of unnecessary items that she hardly ever used. While everyone else in my life seemed to really like me, my Grandma was one of few people that I never really mixed with. My sister was her favorite and she never tried to hide it. It was her often harsh words towards me that I credit with developing a thick skin and not really caring if people did not like me. She was never truly mean to me, but rather harshly blunt without a concern for how things made me feel. It was not until I grew up that I really was able to see and understand her.

Born Lucille Hampton in a shack in Watson, Arkansas, she was the seventh of 16 kids. A rather quiet person, her Mother was very mean to her and showed favor to her other siblings, some of whom would grow to become her biggest rivals in life. To this day she still has a sister that refers to her as "*stuck up*" and "*thinks she's better than me because all of her kids graduated high school and can read.*" The standards are extremely high where I come from.

At the age of 11, her Father's best friend Curley Johnson took an interest in her. He was 47 and smitten. Grandma's Dad objected to the relationship but allowed it to proceed. He believed in his children having the free will to pick who they wanted to be with. Curley proceeded to assist with taking care of her by providing for her, buying her necessities and whatever her heart desired such as bologna and liver cheese, and taking her to town to shop for the latest in Arkansas fashion. At the age of 17, her Mother decided that her sister was more deserving of my Grandfather and tried to intervene to end the relationship, but it did not work. While still dating my Grandfather, my Grandmother started dating a classmate whom she had known her whole life. Shortly after, she found out she was pregnant. Not wanting to marry him, she returned to my Grandfather and married him. She was eight months pregnant when she walked down the aisle or should I say across the room of her family's small shotgun house. She went on to birth 6 more kids after my Aunt Dolly: Curley Jr., Emma, Bernadette, Hosie, James, and Willie, all named after their aunts and uncles- No middle names.

  After marrying, my Grandfather began to distance her from a lot of her family members mainly because of the negativity and poor way they treated my Grandmother. She remained her Father's favorite child until his death. As with most traditional families, my Grandma was the voice and while my Grandpa was the muscle when it came to child rearing. Several years into their marriage, the County Sheriff showed up on her doorsteps and informed her that their marriage was not valid and that my Grandpa had never formally divorced his first wife. He then asked her if she wanted them to arrest him for the crime of bigamy and told her the decision was completely hers. She said "*No*" and 16 years after their first marriage they had wed again, this time it was legal. In 1991, My grandfather died from internal bleeding that proved fatal due to his underlying heart disease.

Never receiving more than an 8th grade education, Grandma continued to work as a housekeeper and cook while working her fingers to the bone to provide for her family. Her kids and friends were her joy, aside from cooking and fishing. As a child, the kids of Lake Village were in awe of her. She was obviously much older than us or our Parents, yet she possessed an athletic ability that was very impressive. One of our favorite pastimes was racing each other in the street. This could be our single activity for the day and was rarely ever interrupted due to hardly any traffic. My Grandma would come out and join us and we would challenge her to race us. She would slowly walk over, shoulders sunken and with what appeared to be a slight limp. Once reaching the starting line, she would kick her shoes off if she had them on, which she rarely did. The race would start and end the same way every time. Grandma wins, and not only would she win, she would oftentimes win by twice as much. No matter how hard we all tried, none of us could beat her and to this day we have never witnessed her losing a race.

At the age of 59, she decided to fulfill a life-long dream and enrolled to get her GED. Virtually illiterate, her dream would require her to freshen up on math and relearn to read. It took her 8 long years but at the age of 67, she accomplished what she set out to do and became a high school graduate. We were all proud of her for this accomplishment.

Her brother John lived there with his family and we lived not far from them. My Mother told us that we were moving to Kansas City, Missouri in a week. *"Where's that?"* I asked, against the idea of moving the moment the words left her mouth. *"It's a city up North. Your uncles all live there and so do some of your grandma's brothers and sisters. You will like it. You got a lot of cousins up there just like here."* She was already rolling her eyes knowing where I was going. I proceeded to interrogate her for the remainder of the evening about *why* we were moving. I did not know anything about Kansas City, but I knew I did not like what I *did* know about cities in general. There were plenty of movies and TV shows that displayed the crime that goes on in the cities and I was not a fan. How could my mother be so OK with moving her two daughters to a city or an area where they may potentially be shot?

> *What about gang violence?*
> *What about me being forced to join a gang?*

I had all these terrible things running through my mind that looking back on them I cannot help but to laugh. It was a reality of my thoughts and the reality of what I have seen so it was all I had to go from. A few weeks later my Mother packed up her car with us in tow and we left my beloved hometown. I can still vividly remember looking out the back window with tears streaming down my eyes as I said my final goodbye. It was dramatic and poetic, but it is so sad for me at the time. I still get that feeling every time I leave Lake

Village even though I know that I would never choose to move back.

After eight long hours, we arrived in the city. While I would not admit this, I was in awe. The city had a lot of beauty to behold; The tall buildings, the big houses, the people dressed all fancy like on an average Tuesday. Then we drove to our new neighborhood. My awe turned to disgust. We pulled up to a house that was close to 54th and Prospect where my uncle June lived. Uncle June was beloved by pretty much everyone in our family. He was a nice old guy, really loving caring and like most of my family- tells it like it is.

That summer we got to hang out with our cousins who we never really got acquainted with prior to our move. We got to go out and explore the city and my Mother made an effort to really highlight a lot of the fun things we would be doing in Kansas City which in hindsight I'm grateful for but I was not won over.

I remember driving the first time I saw the city and the area that we were going to be living in and I remember thinking, *"Why is there so much trash?"*

It seems everywhere I looked, there were chip bags, soda cans, and even ripped open bags of trash. Now do not get me wrong, Lake Village isn't perfect, but this was another level. Not only was I critical of it, I was even more irritated that I had to live in it. For the first few months at my new school which was in walking distance, I carried a plastic Walmart bag with me and picked up trash along the way. Even after making friends and walking to school with them, I continued to do this even though they laughed and told me there was no use. They informed me that there would just be more trash there tomorrow and they were right. I eventually got tired of this and gave it up.

After the summer we moved in with my Mother's boyfriend, Derrick. My sister and I did not take a liking to him very quickly, mainly because we both wanted our Mothers to be with our Fathers, especially me. I have always longed for a two-parent household with my Mother and my Father being together and being married. It wasn't until my teenage years that I realized this wasn't going to be a reality. Well, it was that coupled with the fact that my Mother and Derrick announced their marriage 2 short months later, I was livid. My Mother had always been clear that she was *married to her kids.* It had always just been us and now here he was, interrupting our life and breaking our bond. All our complaints fell on deaf ears, my Mother's decision was made.

For the school year my mother enrolled us into Troost Academy. As usual, I made friends and quickly became one of the student leaders in my grade. One thing I noticed when I got there was that my class was learning things that we had learned in third grade at my school in Arkansas. I told him that I was very bored and that I already knew this stuff and they just shrugged their shoulders. Ultimately, I went on to becoming a "Teacher's Aide" and helped her most of the time. I wasn't required to do most of the assignments because it was pretty clear that I knew the level they were at. Instead of allowing me to move up to the next grade, my school forced me to stay in my grade. It seemed fine at the time but in hindsight I wish there were an effort to move me up at least one grade so that I can be more on level with the things that I already knew.

The next year we moved to Kansas City, Kansas where we lived until my sophomore year of High School. It was during my 6th grade year that my anger issues became prevalent; I had always had a bit of a temper but this year, it really hit the fan.

One day while sitting in class, a male classmate started taunting me and told me he was going to beat me up after school, I told him to do it right now. He proceeded to get up out of his chair, came over to my desk, and slapped me. I then got up and started to fight him. Nothing burns me up more inside then someone putting their hands on me. As I was fighting him and winning by the way, my teacher came over and attempted to break us up. Not aware that it was even my teacher, I began to fight her as well. After I grew tired, I stopped and realized that I had been punching my teacher, leaving bruises on her arms and stomach. I ultimately got expelled for the rest of the year. I was forced to go to an alternative school for the remainder of my sixth-grade year. It was permissible given that there were a lot of kids that were in the same situation and we only had to go to school for three hours a day, but I really look forward to going back to my regular school.

When I went to enroll for my seventh-grade year, they told me that in order for me to come I would have to be participating in anger management for the remainder of my time in the Kansas City, Kansas Public School District. We complied with their request and for 4 years, once a week, I was taken out of class for several hours to meet with my Anger-Management Coach and group to discuss various issues and techniques to combat my anger issues and control my triggers. As much as it annoyed me, I realized the importance of it as I got older. Once I reach a certain level of anger, it becomes hard for me to unwind and calm down.

During my junior year of High School, I got involved in a fight with a classmate after I heard she was talking stuff about me. I simply laughed and said, "*She didn't say anything like that. She's no fool.*" Hearing what was said, she confirmed that she did say it and not only that, she *repeated it*. We went back and forth and before long, it was on! The next thing I knew, a Police Officer was pulling me off her. Our school, like most schools in the inner city, had actual police officers for security. That still did not stop me from trying to get at her. The Officer then pulled out her taser and threatened to tase me if I didn't calm down. Another Officer arrived and they escorted us both into the hallway. Once there, my classmate was left free while both Officers were on me. The second Officer, a short Hispanic man, held my arms behind my back, twisting it. As I tried to ease the pain, my classmate started to run towards me, so I tried even harder to free my arms. I suddenly felt an electric shock go through my body coming from my stomach.

I turned to find the first Officer, a Black woman, looking at me with her taser held near my face. She threatened to turn up the voltage and tase me again if I kept resisting arrest. That shock was enough to bring me to my senses. I complied and then they handcuffed me. Almost immediately, the bell rang, and class was dismissed. I was forced to walk the halls in handcuffs, escorted by two police officers as my classmates looked at me in shock, practically begging for answers as to why someone like me would be in this situation. See, I was not just some regular girl attending school; I was the captain of the volleyball team, editor of the yearbook staff, Editor-in-Chief of the school newspaper, President of the FBLA, a member of the student cabinet, manager for the boys' basketball and baseball team, the voice behind the morning and afternoon announcements, and so much more. I did not deserve this treatment.

    I was ultimately arrested for assault of a Police Officer. The funny thing is, on the way to the police station, she allowed me to ride in the front seat, unhandcuffed- some threat I must have been huh?! My family was livid that I had been taken to adult jail at the age of 17. My case was eventually thrown out due to her not showing up to court three times and my record was expunged.

    Even after graduating high school I have oftentimes enrolled myself into anger management courses and anger management therapy to just deal with certain situations and challenges that I've had to face. To this day I can't recall where my anger issues stemmed from because I was always a fairly happy person.

    For my 13th birthday I got sort of a weird birthday surprise when my Mother announced that she was pregnant. I was of course originally against us but as soon as my little brother arrived in this world our hearts and minds were changed, and we were in love. We were always happy to babysit and care for *DJ*. We would do anything my Mother asked of us. He was the apple of our eye and our little baby. In fact, I do not even recall my Mother and Stepdad spending that much time with him because we always had him. His daycare was across the street from my house and after school I had about three hours to do chores, hang out with my friends, and do homework before I would have had to go pick him up. Instead, I would immediately get my little brother and play with him.

    Looking back, it was so much more than being happy to have a little brother. We also had a nice house and My mother was married, which means that we had a father-figure in the house. Everything seemed to be going well for us. But no matter how good things were on the surface there was still something that I longed for and that I really wanted that seemed unattainable. No matter how much I wanted it or how good I was, I seemed to never be able to have a real relationship with my *own* Father.

Me & My Father | Will Wallace

Chapter 3

I can count on my two hands the number of times that I have seen my Father. From the moment he became a Father he became a deadbeat. Above everything I have ever wanted in my life this has always been at the top of the list; In fact, it has always been my number one. All I have ever wanted was to have a loving relationship with my Father. A relationship where I could be daddy's little girl; A relationship where I really feel like a priority in this life;

A relationship where I did not have to constantly badger and beg for his attention.

I don't recall seeing him much prior to us moving to Kansas City; In fact, I can only remember seeing him for a total of three times, and one of those times I actually got to spend the summer in Dallas with him.

It was perfect. It was everything I wanted and desired from our relationship all wrapped into one summer. He was exactly like I wanted him to be - fun, attentive, and spoiling me rotten. Everywhere I wanted to go and everything I wanted to do- the answer was always *yes*. In hindsight, I now understand what he was doing for a living and that explains why he always had time for me that summer.

My Father was a notorious drug dealer and pimp in Dallas in the Dallas area. He was so notorious that strangers knew of him. One time when I went off to college at University of Arkansas Pine Bluff, I met a guy who said he was from Dallas so asked if he knew my father, Will. He told me the only Will he knew was Will Black, my Father's alias. None of that event mattered because despite all the memories, this summer was the best one I've ever had in my life.

We went shopping, took photos, went to Six Flags, and so much more. Whatever I wanted, I got. I really felt like this was the beginning of the relationship that I have always wanted. Sadly, that feeling was short-lived. He made it clear that while he always acknowledged me as his daughter, he was not interested in having a relationship with me and that really hurt me even to this day. Here I was a person that could win over any and everybody that I encountered yet the one person that I want to fall under my spell never did.

I remember the last time I saw him as a child. He came to visit us in KC and at that time he had taken a job as a truck driver. We met him at a TruckStop, and I was so thrilled. I remember him showing me around the truck. I got behind the steering wheel and was even allowed to honk the horn. When it came time for us to leave, I asked if I could go with him. He said "*No*" and told me that the road was no place for a child, let alone his beautiful little girl. Before we left, he handed me $200 and promised me that he would get me a computer for Christmas since I had been dropping hints left and right. He promised me that he would get it.

Now, my Mother was never the kind of Mother that would sugar-coat things for us. She was always a realist, so we never believed in Santa Claus, the Tooth Fairy, or any childish things of that nature. We knew that she got those gifts on her own and we were grateful and appreciative of that, so there was not any waiting up for Santa Claus or any other make-believe character. On Christmas Day I would simply open my presents waiting for when my Father was going to be there with my computer or to see if he had already given her one. My Mother was always sympathetic to the relationship that I had with Will. It was the one area where she was soft and comforting and always wanted to protect me from, but she never had the heart to tell me the truth. She has never spoken a bad word about him to me. Looking back, I am glad she did because it may have been even worse for me. She never chastised me for running up our phone bill passed $300 multiple times due to my calling him insistently vying for his attention. He always ignored my calls or one of his girlfriends will pick up the phone and tell me that he was not there and that he'll call me back, which he never did. She watched as I continued this one-sided relationship with my Dad, which happened into my teenage years. It was then that I came to realize that this relationship with my Dad was never going to happen; He just did not care enough. My Mother never spanked me or punished me for my use of profanity whenever I was visibly hurt after he had broken yet another promise to me.

    One rare time I was able to get him on the phone, I told him I really want to go spend the summer with him again, like we did that one time because that image of perfection was burned in my brain. He told me that we could make it happen and he gave me a date and told me he will pick me up on that day. I was thrilled yet again for another promising delivery! I was finally going to get to spend some time with my dad and show him that I am a good girl and that I am worthy of his attention, affection, and love. As the days passed, my excitement grew more and more.

    I am usually not one to pack my bags early, but my bags were ready weeks before he was supposed to pick me up. I called and called him trying to reach him by phone prior to the big day but I never got a hold of him. The big day had finally come; The day my Dad was going to come and pick me up and we were going to rekindle our relationship. There I was, sitting on the stairs outside of our house waiting for him to come. My Mother kept coming out and checking on me and asking if I wanted to come in because it was hot outside or if I wanted something to eat- Even food could not bring me into the house. I was waiting for my Dad and he was going to show, he had promised. I watched as cars went by waiting for the moment that a car would pull into the driveway and he would pop out with open arms for me to run into screaming "*Daddy*!" But that moment never came and that dream never manifested. He did not even bother to call and let me know that he wasn't coming. That incident was the final straw for me. He had let me know that he clearly did not want me. I walked into the house and my Mother was standing there. The look in her eyes revealed sympathy. She just hugged me like many times before. As I cried into her arms, I told her it is never going to happen again and that I hated him and that I was never going to do this anymore, and I meant it. From that moment on, I was done. I was moving on with my life and was not going to remain a child living with the hopes of her Dad coming around and being what she wanted him to be.

  At the time of his death, we counted that my Father had at least 13 children. One being my sister, Yvette. Yvette was from Greenville, Mississippi which is right across the Mississippi bridge adjacent to Lake Village. Now, while Will never seemed to want to be bothered with me, he had been clear that he didn't claim Yvette as his own either. One summer I was in Lake Village visiting my family and my Aunt Bee, Will's sister invited me over to her house for a couple of weeks. Aunt

Bee had daughters and Yvette was also invited to stay so that we could bond. Well, they had other plans. For once in my life I was not exactly welcomed. They had their relationships and felt really comfortable leaving me out. They would go to the store and ride bikes and not even bother to ask me if I wanted to come. It just so happened that summer Will came to visit and seemed excited when he saw me. He was pissed to find out that Yvette had also been invited. At the moment he was informed of this she was not there, but it still didn't ease his rage. The next thing I know he grabbed me by my arm and took me to his car throwing me in the backseat. We drove over to Yvette's Mother's house where he hopped out faster than a car to be thrown into park. Yvette and her Mother happened to be sitting on the porch. He hopped out and immediately started yelling at her profanities among other cruel and hurtful things.

"*That little bitch isn't my daughter. I'm so sick and tired of you running around here trying to tell people to tell my family that she's mine. The little ugly ass girl ain't mine because I only make beautiful kids!*" With that, he came to the car and yanked me out of the car by my arm yelling, "*Look at my daughter! She's beautiful! That little ugly ass bitch is not my daughter, so you need to stop fucking filling her head with those lies.*"

Her Mother screamed back at him telling him that she was his daughter and that he knew it and he needed to step up and be a better Father, but it fell on deaf ears. He pushed me back in the car, got back in the driver seat, and pulled off. I remember looking at

Yvette the whole time. I felt more sorry for her than I did for myself. The look of sadness on her face was unlike anything I have ever seen before. After a few days, my Father left to go back to Dallas and Yvette could come back over with me and my cousins. This time instead of leaving me out, they begin to taunt and tease me. I spoke a little more properly than they did, and I was teased for it. It's funny because a lot of kids in KC teased me for my thick country accent. They started calling me other names and followed me to the room that I was staying in as I was trying to get away from them. I finally turned around and got Yvette's face and said, *"That's why my daddy don't want your little ugly ass!"*

    Her face went back to the face of sadness but this time I did not care. I had not one drop of sympathy for her this time. She brought this on herself. I knew exactly what to say to trigger her emotions. She ran into the living room crying, my cousin's in tow. After that I was asked to go back to Lake Village.

    Fast forward about 12 years later, Yvette and I had established more of a relationship. We were talking on the phone at least once a month and sometimes more. One day she called me and sounded unusually cheery. I asked her what was going on and she explained that she had gotten a call from our Father. I rolled my eyes and asked why that would make her happy. He had called her to talk about them and their relationship. She explained to me that he called to apologize to her for the way he treated her as a child and for not being there for her. He said he wanted to establish a relationship with her going forward and he wanted to change things. I was about 24 years of age when this happened and although it had been over 10 years since, I declared to not give a damn about him. I could not help but to wait for my phone call because I could not wait to hear this apology. But it never happened. He never once picked up the phone to apologize to me the way that he had did to her. This has only infuriated me more because he knew without a shadow of a doubt that I was his daughter.

    In the fall of 2013, I received a pleasant surprise. I woke up to find a friend request on Facebook from Will. Without hesitation, I accepted it. After accepting his friend request, I then received a phone call from him saying he wanted us to be friends. I felt obliged but still had my guard up, given our history. We went on to establish a pretty decent relationship. I made a note to never call him so that each time we talked it was due to him reaching out to me. He called a lot and we talked about everything under the sun. Politics was a frequent topic. He would call every time I posted something political on Facebook. He shared his republican views with me which kind of shocked me.

    That November, he called me and asked if I wanted some money for my birthday. Who would say no to that, right? We proceeded to just have a general conversation and when I had to get off the phone to go to work, he stopped me and proceeded to tell me something that I've been longing for him to say.

> He said that he loved me and that he was very proud that I didn't disappoint him with how smart I was.

I was so shocked. All these times I've never ever heard him say that he loved me. To this day it is still the best birthday present I have ever received. After that, the calls continued. We were talking on the phone through all hours of the night. There wasn't a topic that we didn't discuss including the summer that I had spent with him.

Now I grew up on a pretty big lake but today, as an adult, I have a fear of water that I do not remember having as an incredibly young child. In fact, we spent countless unsupervised hours in the lake swimming and hanging out. One day we were having a conversation and he asked if I had a boyfriend. I said of course. Truthfully, I am always dating people, but I did not believe in monogamy. But what I did not tell him about was the role that he played in that philosophy. He then said something that was a little strange to me. He said he remembered that I used to like those little white boys. Confused, I asked what he was talking about. He said he remembered the day he saved me from drowning. I just got through looking at this little white boy and he came over and y'all started flirting. He quickly broke it up and told me if I ever dated a white man that he would disown me. That was a funny statement since I've never felt like he ever owned me. But something he said stood out to me- I almost drowned?

I've always had this dream where I was standing in water and all of a sudden I get swept into the water and I'm fighting to get above water but all these waves were coming at me so I was never able to gain my footing. Every time it felt like I was close, another wave would come and then I would wake up.

He went on to tell me that he was watching me play in the pool at the waterpark we were visiting when he turned away for a second and I had disappeared. Frantic, he rushed over to where he last saw me and began to look for me. After what seemed like an eternity, he found me. He grabbed me by my bathing suit and pulled my lifeless body out of the pool. Once out, he laid me down and performed CPR. After a few attempts, I coughed up water and came back to life, I was in shock. I could not believe that this was something that really had happened to me. What is more shocking is that I cannot believe this was not something that changed him for the better.

I chose to overlook that and move on with our new founded relationship. In March of 2014, I was invited to a political conference in Dallas. I told him about it and asked if we could see each other. He agreed and on the last day of the conference it was time to see him. It had been 16 years since I had last seen him. By this time, he had gone through years of gaining and losing weight. He had recently had an incident where some of the guys that worked for him and some of his whores robbed him of everything, he had beat him mercilessly until he was close to death. That coupled with drug use over the years left him on many prescription drugs.

That night, I was knocking on his door. My butterflies in my stomach were killing me. His roommate answered. He led me into the room where my Dad was. He looked very different, he wasn't as lively and as bright as he always was. It appeared that he had lost his charisma. He came over and hugged me. I did not hug him back. All these horrific memories of the past started to come back to my head. I was finally standing in the room with him and I had so much stuff that I wanted to say to him, yet the words would not come out of my mouth. I am usually a tough cookie, but I completely folded when facing him.

For the next 30 minutes I had what is perhaps the most awkward conversations I have ever been a part of. The relationship we were having on the phone did not translate when we were in person. I suddenly became unenthusiastic and really did not want to be there with him. All those memories as a child came rushing back to me and I began to chastise myself for letting him in so easily. I wanted to still have the conversation that I really desired to have with him. I do not remember what we talked about. I just know there were so many things that I wanted to say but my pride and emotions would not let me. I would never describe myself as a coward, but I *was* that day. I left shortly afterwards, not knowing that it would be the last time that I would ever see him alive.

After I returned home our phone conversations and relationship continued. He still called a lot and wanted to continue a relationship with me but a part of me was over it. Not necessarily all because of him but because I had a moment to finally address everything, yet I did not muster up the balls to do so.

Towards the end of July in 2014, his wife called me and informed me that he was in the hospital. I thought nothing of it but asked her to keep me updated on what is going on. I just thought it was a routine and that they will figure it out and he will be fine. Later that night she called me back and told me that he had in fact died. I was in shock; I was hurt; I was angry.

How could I start to get what I've always desired and then have it taken away from me so abruptly? We were supposed to talk that day and now he was dead. He saved a lot of who I am particularly with my relationship with men. He has been both a good and bad part of my life and I was so angry at God for taking him especially at a time like this. I had gotten so close to establishing his relationship with him that I could not believe that this was ending just like this. In hindsight, I was given one more final time to see him and to have that conversation, but I just could not bring myself to do it. Primarily, because I thought I had more time to discuss these things with him but as it turned out I didn't. I did not get the chance to say goodbye and express how I really felt. I Did not get an opportunity to release all the pain and anger that was locked up inside of me and it's my fault that I never got the chance to talk about it. I do not think it's a child's fault when a parent does not want them or does not choose to establish a relationship with them. What I blame on myself is the fact that I had an opportunity to have a sit-down conversation with him and I chose not to. I do not have many regrets in my life but if there is one thing that I regret, it's not having that conversation with him when I had the chance to. You never know when it is going to be your last time seeing someone or talking to someone until it is.

Me & My High School Friends

Chapter 4

Growing up we were never spoiled children. My Mother raised us to be very well-mannered and very respectful, which made us overall good kids. We didn't get a lot of spankings nor did we get yelled at a lot, but we just knew that we were going to behave. My sister and I knew when my Mother would say yes or no to something before we even asked, so most of the time we never even bothered. But there was one area where my Mother never said no- Food.

By the age of 7, my belly was poking out over my pants. My Mother never put any limit on anything we ate nor how much of it we ate. See, my Mother was always pretty thin her whole life. She wasn't the best cook even though she was raised in the south by traditional family, so we ate out a lot. McDonald's was a staple in our household as well as Chili's, Applebee's, IHOP, Denny's, and many others. We indulged in fast-food very single week. So, it's no surprise that my sister and I were pretty overweight as young children. Even then, my Mother still never said no or put limits on our food for us. It was never really a problem for me although I didn't realize that I was bigger than most of the kids I have encountered. It wasn't until I had reached my teen years that I really saw the difference in size between my sister and our peers.

Kids at school would crack the occasional joke but It never really bothered me. What other people thought of me never really seemed to bother me very much, but it was always what I thought of myself that took up all the space in my head. Whereas other girls were beginning to come into themselves and remain feminine, I was kind of a shrank away; Not in size, although I wish. I begin to dress like a tomboy. I wore baggy clothes at least two sizes too big thinking that it would hide the fact that I was extremely overweight. But it just further revealed it. By the time I reached the age of 15, I was experiencing full-blown low self-esteem. It is still the darkest time of my life even considering everything I have been through since then. I hated myself and everything that came with it. I hated the fact that I felt unwanted by my Dad and longed for the love that I would never get from him. But most of all I just hated my life. Yes, I was popular and had guys that were trying to talk to me. I even had the occasional little boyfriends. I was also captain of the volleyball team and excelled in that sport and as well as others, like track. Despite all of this, I could not really think of a lot of positive things about my life. So instead of talking to people, I just talked to myself more and more, eventually falling into depression. I got to the point where I always wanted to be alone in my room and ultimately got to the point where I just wanted it all to be over. And that is when my suicidal thoughts began to happen.

    I don't remember the first time I had a thought of ending my life, but I do know that there were many thoughts about it. I knew that I wanted out of life, and out of this situation I was in. We didn't have a gun in the house, but I knew where I could easily access one. But to me, guns were for protecting yourself and hunting so that thought was quickly pushed out of my mind as soon as it entered it.

    I knew of some girls at my high school who were cutters and I started talking to them. They had two friends who have committed suicide through cutting, and they were a group of depressed and sad girls. They cut their arms, legs, and thighs. Basically, any part of their body that they could get away with without it being wildly noticeable. So, I began to hang out with them. They talked about hurting as if it was a drug. To them, it was an escape from the world and with every slice that would offer a high to them that would allow them to temporarily escape whatever situation they were facing at that time that was causing them anguish. I eventually grew to want to feel it. Looking back this had to be the dumbest thought I have ever had in my life. I sought them out for a reason, so it was not necessarily a following thing but more of an inquisitive thing of wanting to know more about doing this to myself. I had read about it in magazines and such and was curious as to how this felt although it never really seemed to make a full connection in my brain.

  A few days later I got a razor from one of them. I had a towel handy to cut over and to stop the bleeding. I gave myself a pep talk and said it as I sat on my bed. I held my right arm over the towel and dug the razor into my arm. The pain that I felt immediately after completely brought me back to reality. Nobody was home and if they had been, I don't think my reaction would've been any different. I screamed at the top of my lungs. Why did I ever think this is going to make me feel better? But I tried it and I still have the scar to prove it. I have oftentimes looked down at the scar and laughed at myself. I waited until the scar virtually stopped bleeding and put on a Band-Aid. The next day I marched up to those girls at school and proceeded to give them a speech about how this is really painful, and it makes no sense. I didn't realize how pissed I was until that moment. They stood there looking at me, mouth ajar. It's funny after I spoke with them and got off my soapbox, the three of the nine girls actually stopped cutting themselves that day. See, I'm a helper. I tried to end my own life and ended up saving someone else's.

The problem still existed though; I still wanted to escape from life but cutting myself wasn't going to do it. But then another idea came to me - Pills. I drafted up my next plan. I came up with a date that I will do it and the next morning I was not going to wake up. Two weeks before my date I went on a goodbye tour. I visited all of my best friends at home and hung out with them one last time and made sure we did whatever it was that they wanted to do, even if it was something that I hated. I did all the silly annoying things my little sister wanted me to do. I was very obedient and did all my chores. I wanted everyone to be happy and to accept my decision and to understand that this is what I wanted, and I just didn't want to be here anymore. But I also wanted them to be happy and to have a happy final memory of me.

That's something about me- Even when I'm going through my hardest times, I am still constantly thinking of other people and how I can positively affect their lives. On my goodbye tour, I also started collecting prescription pills. I would ask to use the bathroom to go and I would have a Ziploc bag that I kept in my backpack where I would take about half of the pill prescription pills in the medicine cabinet and pour them into the Ziploc bag. My parents were not prescription pill users, so I knew I didn't have enough in our house to take but I also knew I had to get it from somewhere else. One day I woke up and it was the big day, my final day.

The final day went smoothly. I did the same thing I had been doing for weeks, making sure everyone had a great time with me and making sure I was an obedient perfect little child. The night before bed I said a prayer and asked for forgiveness. I asked that everyone around me would understand and accept my decision. After everyone went to bed, I proceeded to take all the pills one by one. I remember exactly how many there were, but I know I stopped counting around 60 or 70. I just wanted the process to be over. I didn't want to wake up and realize that my plan failed. I needed to escape this place of hell that was in my head. I needed to escape my thoughts of not being good enough to myself. When I was done, I laid down on my back and looked up at my ceiling until I fell asleep hoping it was my last time ever that I would fall asleep. Well, obviously I did not die.

    The next day I woke up in excruciating pain. I had never experienced such pain in my life. I remember being bent over and just throwing up a colored liquid. I could not believe how much pain I was in. When my Mother found me, I was throwing out what seemed like all my intestines. While we were not people who were quick to rush to the hospital for every little incident, her immediate reaction was to take me to the hospital- No way!

    I told her I didn't need to go to the hospital but that I just needed to lay down a little bit and I'm sure I'll be fine. I couldn't bear the shame of my Mother learning that I had attempted suicide. I had also researched enough to know that they would inform my family of what I have done and would pump my stomach in order to get all the pills out. As everyone in my family left to go on about their day, I lied in bed thinking about how maybe this wasn't the time for me to go. That didn't stop me from attempting to do the same thing about a year later with even more pills. I got the same results - A tummy ache and disappointment in myself for not being able to accomplish this. This time I stopped to evaluate what I was doing and why. Well, I knew why I was doing it and I knew what I was doing. Since I failed twice at the same thing, I was confused as to where I want to do next with life.

      At the time, my Mother was allowing me to read Cosmopolitan Magazine. One day I came across an article called, *"Fake it till you make it."* In the article, the Author took you through steps to fake your self-confidence and high self-esteem until you actually achieved it. Instead of taking another attempt at suicide, I decided that this is what I was going to do. The thought of loving myself never crossed my mind but here it was in plain sight. Over the next few months, I incorporated the lessons I read about into my everyday life. Whenever I had a negative thought, I would quickly replace it with something positive. Although I still dressed like a tomboy, I broke my body down into little pieces and only focused on the things I liked. I spoke extremely high of myself to others. I poured myself into all the positive areas of my life. I prayed a lot for healing a fulfillment.

Chapter 5

In the spring of 2007, I moved to Belleville, Illinois to be closer to my family. My Mother and Father had moved there a few years prior and I wanted to spend a little time with my family. I was about 16 when I left Kansas City and I stayed with my Uncle James after that. In my senior year of high school, I accomplished a goal that I set for myself at a young age and managed to get my own apartment. I was so excited.

After graduating high school that May, I decided to attend the University of Arkansas Pine Bluff which is an HBCU. I was very excited to be able to attend a historically black college and university especially since this was in my home state and near my hometown. I had a wonderful experience being engulfed in black culture at UAPB and I would not change it for the world. After my first semester, I was less than thrilled with college. Although I was having a lot of fun, I just did not feel the college experience was for me and I wanted to take a break. I ultimately would attend another college after I moved to Kansas City and switched my major from journalism to political science. We will talk more about that in another chapter.

During my time at UAPB and after moving to Belleville, I was experimenting a lot in party life. Like most kids my age, I partied into the wee hours of the morning and I loved it. To me I was living the life that I wanted at that point and as long as I was able to afford it myself, I didn't see a problem with it; For the things that I couldn't afford, there were always guys for that.

I found my own apartment in Illinois and told myself that I would stay there for about a year and then I would return back to Kansas City. One day, shortly after moving in, as I was sitting on my phone listening to the radio, a guy approached me. He was nice and tall, like I liked with beautiful dark-brown skin. He told me that his name was "*D*" and that he thought that I was the most beautiful woman he has ever met. I mean who could blame him?

He told me that he wanted to take me out the next day and that he was single and looking to settle down. Now, I was never the "*settling down*" type of girl and it has only been recently that I have ever even had that desire of myself. I felt obliged to take him up on the offer being that he was nice and handsome. The next day he picked me up a little earlier than I thought. We were not scheduled to go out until 5pm, yet he picked me up around 12pm noon. He told me that he couldn't stay away and that he really wanted to take me shopping. I found it to be weird, but I didn't decline his offer. Now, at this time I was still pretty much a tomboy and didn't care that much about clothes and shoes but do you think I was foolish enough to tell somebody that who was willing to buy them for me?

So, shopping we went. He took me to the mall and to multiple stores spending about $1000. The shopping trip would become a recurring theme in my dating life. I would meet a guy and he would just want to take me shopping. So, who am I to get in the way of their pursuit of happiness, right? After shopping he took me to some fancy steakhouse in St. Louis. It was wonderful and he was a lot of fun. He was charismatic and charming. He reminded me of my Dad in a lot of ways. That should have been my first warning.

We spent a lot of time together and he was very giving. Then our relationship started to take a turn for the worse. One day on my way home , I drove by his house and I saw him sitting outside on the porch with another girl. It wouldn't have been a big deal had the girl not been sitting between his legs. Afterwards, he came over to my house not aware that I saw him. Once I confronted him, he got to explaining away and told me what I really saw. In typical Cecilia fashion, I pretended to be hurt and pretended as if I really cared when I actually didn't. I was seeing other guys at the time and although he had said he was looking for a monogamous relationship, I thought I did not. But apparently, we were on the same page.

I forgave and we moved. About two months later, we had yet another incident with another girl. His sister had a friend that was interested in him and he started to date her. He told me that it was because she was willing to "*break bread*" (which meant she helped with the money and did what was asked of her). Again, I didn't really care much but pretended to in order to get another reaction. While I was having a lot of fun with him, I didn't necessarily see a long-term relationship or marriage in our future, so I was pretty much kind of going with the flow. And then the flow stopped.

Around that time, I had an exceptionally large amount of guy friends. We would hang out and party a lot. I was often a *wing-man* for them but I didn't care. I was always VIP, got to meet a lot of local celebrities, and never had to pay for anything. I never asked him what he thought of this because frankly I didn't care about his opinion. Plus, it was not going to change the fact that I liked hanging out with my guy friends and sometimes even more than my girlfriends. One day when I had two girlfriends over spending the night, I heard a knock at the door. I went to answer, and it was a member of our group holding up a mutual friend of ours. They expressed that he was drunk, had lost his keys, and had nowhere to go. Their girlfriends would not allow him to spend the night at their house, so I was really the last resort. I thought nothing of it and let him come in. I got him a glass of water and a trash can in case he decided to throw up in the middle of the night and went back to bed.

I woke up the next morning to what sounded like the Feds at my door. I answered it and it was a D. He seemed really pissed off. Apparently while I was asleep, my friend started to harass my girlfriends. They both have boyfriends that were friends with my boyfriend and one of them called their boyfriend to tell him what happened. After he picked her up, he informed my boyfriend of what was going on. He was unlike anything I've ever seen from him. He was on his way to work and was in such a rage. He grabbed me by my collar and pushed me against the wall yelling in my face. He said that he couldn't believe that I was cheating on him and that I had a guy in my house and now all of our business was out in the streets. That was nowhere near the case yet that was what he wanted to believe so he did. He stormed out as I tried to explain the real situation, but he was not hearing any of it.

That day I blew his phone up trying to get him to understand what actually happened and to explain to him that the guy was actually a friend and not someone that I was seeing, which was the truth. All of my calls went unanswered. I then proceeded to go to work. When I got home, he and his friends were partying in an empty lot near my house. I walked over to see what was going on. There he stood with his sister's friend who he had claimed was only interested in him. I walked up to confront him, and he noticed that he had a fifth of Gin that was almost empty in his hand. It is apparent that he had been drinking. At this point, his drinking never really was a problem because if he was drinking, so was I. I walked up to him and asked what was going on. He started laughing at me and proceeded to tell me everything. I told him that I no longer cared.

I started to back away and before I could turn around, he came towards me and slapped me. I was in shock. I had never had a man just hit me, so it was a little hard for me to process. But he didn't stop there. As I stood there trying to wrap my brain around this, he drop-kicked me in my chin. His friends rushed him and told him that he was tripping, and he needed to stop. I backed up and walked home. As I sat in my house, my blood just started to boil over. Who the hell did he think he was putting his hands on me? I had watched my Mother get abused when I was a child so this really started bothered me. I went to my kitchen, grabbed a knife, and went out on my porch. I was waiting for him to walk by on the way to his house. I was hoping that he would be alone and lo and behold about five minutes later he was walking home to his house alone.

>He saw me and said, *"What the fuck do you want?"*

>*"Do you think you can just put your hands on me and we're just gonna be cool?",* I said.

>*"Bitch I'll put my hands on you again",* he said.

And he did. He walked up to me and proceeded to swing on me. Being a fighter myself, I stood my ground as we proceeded to fight in the middle of the street and in front of my house. It was not until a few minutes later that he saw the knife in my hand. He took a step back. He looked hurt.

> *"You really gonna stab me?"*, he asked.

> *"Hell yeah I was! You are tripping! You don't just put your hands on me and get away with it! But you know what? I'm done. I'm not gonna fight you. We're done."*, I said.

I turned around to walk into my house. As I reached the door to enter my house, I felt him behind me. I turned around just as he grabbed me by my neck and forced me into my house. He turned and locked the door.

The next 30 minutes of my life with sheer horror. Still grabbing me by the throat, he threw me into the floor and proceeded to punch and slap me in my face. I tried to fight back but after about 15 minutes all the fighting I had seemed to have left my body. I had worn myself out. But it seemed as if he was just getting started. He proceeded to pound my face, choke me until I almost passed out, and then he slapped me. I was somehow able to break free from him. As I struggled to stand on my feet and go for the door, he picked up my iron and threw it at my back, hitting me square in my back. I also had a wooden stick in my house that I kept over my door just in case of an emergency. He grabbed it and started beating me with it after kicking me back to the floor. Blood was leaking from my face, but I still had to use my arms to protect it as he aimed for it with the stick.

    I could not believe what was going on. I never thought I would ever be in a situation like this. He then stood me up and forced me against the wall. Then he suddenly stopped. The look on his face had changed. It went from anger to attraction. He looked as if he just saw me for the first time in his life. He started to caress my face and tell me how beautiful I was. He told me that he could not live without me and that he loved me. He then ripped my shirt off of me along with my bra. I was confused and trying to fight him off but even in his new emotional state, he was still much stronger than me. He started to kiss me on my neck and my chest and begun telling me that I was sexy. He explained that he was so lucky to have a woman like me. My mind had started racing. My body was still too weak to fight him off completely, so I still struggled. He then grabbed me by my hair and dragged me into my bedroom, tossing me onto the bed. He then climbed into bed with me. He wrapped his arms around me and started to kiss me, but I bit his tongue. He punched me a couple times in the face and told me to stop fighting the love he wanted to give me. He proceeded to rip my pants off along with my underwear. This time I was screaming for help and for him to stop. He had this really crazy look on his face with really dark, black eyes. He kept telling me that he loved me and that he could not live without me. I continued to scream and tried to push him off me, beating him on his arm. But nothing stopped him. He had made his mind up about what he was going to do to me. He turned my body over; my objecting screams being ignored. He opened my legs and proceeded to sodomize me. The pain was excruciating. The more I struggled, the harder he went. He wrapped his arm around my neck, telling me to shut up and take it.

> *"I know you like it so stop fighting it",* he yelled in my ear.

While I have done a lot of immature things in our relationship as I did with every man that I have ever encountered, this was crazy. As he sodomized me, he continued to tell me that he loved me, and he could never live without me. I eventually went numb. I stopped screaming and crying hysterically.

I had just laid there, hoping that he would soon finish. After what seemed like a lifetime, he did. The kisses continued as he laid on top of me, covered in sweat and breathing heavily. Then, he simply got up and left. I tried to pull myself out of bed, but my body was in so much pain. The fight left my body extremely sore. I eventually fell asleep crying in my bed, not able to move a great deal of my body. After waking up the next day, I went to my bathroom to look at myself in the mirror. I was left with large bruises all over my body and red knots on my face. I had barely recognized myself. The right side of my face was badly swollen, and I was embarrassed for anyone to see me that way. While I knew it was not my fault when it happened to me, I still proceeded to see him. I had let him inside of my house and inside of my life. I felt I should have known better. After all, this wasn't my first time being violated.

Back in my hometown of Lake Village, Arkansas, I was left in charge of babysitting the kids at an incredibly young age. There was a limit to the number of children I could babysit. I couldn't babysit no more than five kids and I was pretty good at taking care of them. I was very mature for my age and my family had raised me to be very self-sufficient. Many people did not have a problem leaving their child with a child, even babies. But when I was not in charge of babysitting or whenever too many children were present, we hand someone else up as our children.

Jake was a friend of the family and someone pretty much everyone in our hometown knew and trusted. He was an older man and was very respected. He was left in charge of babysitting the children while the parents went out and partied or went to the boat. I don't recall when it first happened, but I do know around the time I was five years old, Jake entered into a relationship with me. Allow me to explain.

For as long as I can remember, Jake had always expressed his feelings for me. He used every stolen moment that we had to tell me that I was his girlfriend and he was my boyfriend and that when I was old enough, he was going to marry me. He was always telling me how much he loved me and that we were going to be together forever. He had to be around 50 at the time. He would always sneak little gifts when no one was watching. Whether it was some candy, a small toy that would go unnoticed or a flower that he picked for me, he was no stranger to expressing his love through gifts. He wrote me little love notes and made me promise to rip up and throw it in the trash after reading it. He was also having sex with me. Somewhere between the ages of 5 and 8, he was brainwashing me. He would always make it clear that we didn't have sex, we made love. He was always very affectionate with me and anything I asked and the next. We were bonded together forever. Whenever the other kids were napping, he would have sex with me. He was always constantly reminding me that our relationship had to remain a secret and that I couldn't tell anyone, or I would hurt my Mother. And I believe them.

    I always looked at my Mother as one of the greatest people ever even from a young age and I don't want to hurt her, so I kept my mouth shut. It was never ending and only stopped when I moved away. I kept the secret of me being violated as a child to myself. It wasn't something I shared with anyone which is why I'm surprised that I'm willing to share it in this book. I never intended to include this in here. A friend of mine, who had gone through similar experiences, encouraged me to finally get this off my chest. It took a lot of convincing on her end as I've never really spoken about it, but I decided that she was right. I needed to let this out as this was the final part of my healing from it.

    I have come to terms with what he did to me and how it has affected me. I acknowledge that it has affected a lot of things in my life, particularly my outlook on relationships. What Jake stole from me was more than just my innocence and virginity. He also stole the desire to have a relationship with someone. As I got older and most of my friends went to the periods of having boyfriends and as did I, I never could feel anything for anybody. I didn't really consider any real relationship because I didn't believe in monogamy and I couldn't really experience intimacy. No matter how much they expressed that they loved me, wanted to be with me, and wanted to build a future with me, I was always clear that I didn't see this going anywhere, not then or ever. I tried really hard at times to feel but I just couldn't. And Jake took that from me. But It wasn't just him.

    When I moved to Camden to stay with my Grandmother, I had another experience of being violated. My cousin Ebony was a teenager and she was very cool in my eyes. As an adult now, I realize that she really was just a person that drank too much back then but as a child, she always seemed very lively and I wanted to spend as much time with her as I could. I don't recall what happened to her parents as she passed away so long ago. I just remembered that she stayed with her Grandmother and her boyfriend.

    Boy was he nice. He always seemed to go above and beyond to show me how I was his favorite amongst all of my cousins. We would go up to him asking him for a dollar and he gave it to us, but he would give me more than everyone else. While others got only $1, he would give me $20. It felt like a lot of money to a young me. He would always tell me that I was special and that I had the right amount of baby fat. No matter what, he would always find a time or moments where he can talk to me alone. He would always tell me that I had to be the smartest one in my class. He was very encouraging. I just looked really smart and really special. Several months later, I decided to spend the night over Ebony's house. I didnt think anything of his behavior at the time because I was just a child.

That night I was up late flipping through the TV watching infomercials, one of my favorite things to watch. I heard someone come downstairs. I thought nothing of it and continued to watch my infomercials. It was him. He had got a glass of water and turned the light off in the kitchen when he was finished. He came and sat at the foot of the couch that I was laying on. He asked what I was doing, and I answered him. He scooted up on the couch getting closer to me and then he proceeded to tell me once again how special I was and that I was going to do great things in my life. A beautiful girl like me with my smarts and talents is bound to go places. He placed his hand on his shoulder and slowly slid it down my arm. The next thing I knew, he had placed his hand in my shirt which he found my small, child-breasts. I pushed his hand away and asked him what he was doing. He stopped, smiled, and said he was just having a little fun.

> "*You mean to tell me after all the money that I've given you and how nice I am to you, I can't have a little fun with you?*", he asked.

Even though I knew it was wrong just as well as Jake, I understood the logic in what he was saying. He leaned over and started kissing me. He left a lingering smell that I would never forget even to this day even though I don't remember what he looked like. He could walk right in front of me and I would not know who he was. He put his hand up my shirt and this time, I didn't stop him. He started telling me how I smelled so good, better than he thought I'd smell. I just laid there. He lifted up my shirt and his kisses traveled down my chest and my stomach. He slowly pulled down my pants and underwear. He was whispering how long he waited to do this and that he wanted to do it from the moment he laid eyes on me. I chose not to scream or shout. I had just laid there and let him do what he wanted.

  This activity had seemed to go on for hours and he was sweating profusely. By the time he was done, the front side of my shirt was soaked with his sweat. He continued to kiss me while telling me that he knew I was special and that he had a good time with me. He got up, pulled up his pants, and went upstairs and lay down as if nothing happened.

  I didn't sleep for the rest of the night. Early that morning, I went back to my Grandma's house and took a shower, trying to get the smell of him off me. I never ever went back over Ebony's house again and never saw him again to my recollection.

  Again, I kept my mouth shut. While I never blamed myself for what happened to me as a child because I knew this was something that they weren't supposed to be doing, I didn't bring myself to tell anybody. With D, I wanted to tell someone what happened to me. The next day, one of his friends informed me that he had been arrested. D had already been to prison and was out on parole. Early that morning his Parole Officer had declared him in violation of his parole, had him arrested, sending him back to prison. He was forced to serve several more years before being released.

    About seven years ago, I was discussing the story with a friend and she asked me what happened to him. I explained to her that I honestly did not know. All this time I had never thought about him or what happened. I had just buried it in the back of my mind with everything else. I told her his name, which is a very uncommon name, and she looked him up. His name was Deltorian Jones.

    "*He's dead*", she said. She read that he was killed a couple years ago. He was stabbed to death by his sister's boyfriend while playing a card game.

    Good riddance! He didn't deserve to be alive after he had done to me and someone else. After he was sent back to prison, I came home to a letter from him. He acted as if everything was normal. He said he missed me and sent information for me to come visit him as if nothing had happened. I was appalled. The next day I went over to a friend's house and looked him up. There it was on the screen, "*Sex Offender*" in big, bold, red letters above his name. I sent him a letter telling him that I looked at that and saw that he was a sex offender. I also told him about what he had done to me that night and that this would be his last ever hearing from me and that I hoped he rotted in prison before going to Hell. Next week, he sent a letter back telling me his version of what I know is a lie.

According to him, he had a friend back in his hometown of Milwaukee who had a little sister that had a crush on him. He said she was always flirting with him despite the age difference. He was 16 and she was 12. One day, he went to go visit his friend. His sister answered the door and informed him that his friend hadn't come home yet but he could wait inside, so he did. He said his sister then started to flirt with him once again and practically threw herself at him. He said he repeatedly told her "No." Hurt, she told her brother and parents that he had raped her. He was later arrested and charged with raping her. He was eventually found guilty and sentenced to prison.

He also said that he remembered nothing about that night between us. He said he had blacked out and he doesn't remember anything that happened the night after he had a couple drinks with his friends. I read the letter and then burned it. After that, I didn't think much of him.

While everyone that experiences sexual abuse to some extent especially child abuse or child sexual abuse has different reactions, I had to really face mine in order to overcome my fear of intimacy and to realize how messed up I was when it came to relationships with men. I am happy to say that I finally healed. Thanks to counseling with my first lady, I was able to work through a lot of what happened to me as a child and come up with a plan of action to change the way I acted as an adult because of it. I want you to understand that this is not easy for me to talk about; It is not easy for anybody to talk about. Sexual violation is a very painful thing no matter how well or poorly someone seems to cope with it. We all cope with it at our own pace and in our own ways. For those of you that have experienced something similar to what I have, my heart and soul goes out to you. I pray that you find the healing that you need to overcome what has happened to you. No, you'll never be the same no matter what age it happens or whose hands it is at. Yes, your life is changed forever. But does it have to mean that you have to live in darkness forever? No! Truth be told, the desire to escape away from what happened to me as a child was a part of the reason that I wanted out of my life. I wanted to end the thoughts and the dreams that came with them.

  I wish I had learned to cope with the main part of the reason I wanted out, because that would allow me to be truly happy. And while I didn't cope with it instantly, I worked through my issues when it happened to me and I could only hope that others can do the same.

  See, there are always clues that come before someone does something like this and it's up to you whether you decide to stay, or you decide to leave. And I truly hope that you make the decision to leave because the longer you stay, the harder that it will get to leave and the deeper they will get into that state with you. You deserve better but you will not get it until you realize it.

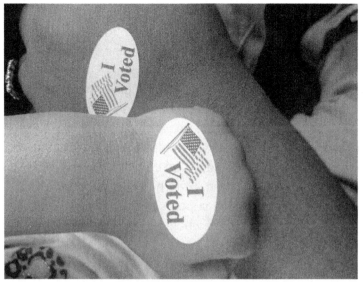

Amelia's First Time Voting

Chapter 6

In April of 2008, I decided I needed to change. After what I just experienced, I realized I needed to get away from this area to distance myself from him and that situation. I decided it was time to go back home. No, not to leave Arkansas but to Kansas City. I packed my bags and on April 1st of that year, I took the train back home. Within a matter of days of returning, all was well. I just felt better to be back. I moved in with a friend of mine and returned to my job that I had held while in high school.

Almost a month later I was with my friend at Walgreens, when I had another eye-opening experience about my life. She was getting a prescription filled because she had contracted another STD from her boyfriend. I started looking through magazines to pass time and while picking up a national magazine that was geared toward the black community, I begin to scrutinize the published content. Almost supernaturally, the magazine landed on a specific page. On it and at the center was an incredibly attractive black man in a suit. If you know anything about me, when it comes to men in suits- it's like lingerie to men. Here he is, as handsome as he wanted to be, and my superficial side determined that he must be an expert on whatever he was talking about.

So, I decided to read the article. The title was something along the lines of, "*Why I'm a Black Republican.*" I thought it a little odd because Black people just are not Republicans. Sure, they had Condoleezza Rice and Colin Powell, but they reached our quota. Just how many of us did they need?

I wasn't into politics whatsoever at this point in my life. I was only 20 years old, so I was of age to participate in only one election. It was back when I was in Illinois and a guy came knocking saying that he was running for some office and needed me to vote for him. I almost closed the door on him as I told him that I didn't care anything about politics. He stopped me and said that he really wanted to change the community for the better and that we needed new leadership. He also said that he would give me a ride to the polls if I would just vote for him, so I agreed. A week later, a van came to pick me up along with numerous other people in my neighborhood, taking me to the polls. I didn't think it was a big deal or that it would really change anything. I just knew that the guy seemed like a fairly good guy and had a passion for people, so why not give him a chance to win this office.

    I don't recall his name nor what his political side was nor what position he was running for. What I did know was that I was just being kind and giving my due diligence for the community and I was done for the day. That was my first and only political experience. It was a completely ignorant experience void of any knowledge and research. Looking back, I wouldn't change it for the world. It allows me to see how so many people, no matter what community they are in, get lost in the political process. The truth is it can be very overwhelming if you're not a politico or working in politics of some aspect. And that is what I was.

    As I read the article further, I found out that he was like me- raised in a single-parent household and raised in inner-city. He saw certain issues in our community that he wanted to change and felt that the conservative platform could do that. As I read it, I found myself mentally checking off things that I agree with in this article. As of this moment, I do not remember the article verbatim and I didn't even bother to buy the magazine. I do remember that he touted his support for small businesses and felt that was a way to pull a lot of our community out of poverty. He also felt we needed a better education system, something that I couldn't agree with more.

I graduated in 2006 from Central High School, one of the worst-performing schools in the state of Missouri. After getting into politics I was watching a political documentary and found my alma mater was featured on it. They were talking about schools that received a lot of funds, yet the academics were abysmal. I agreed with this man wholeheartedly.

Later that night, I went to Wikipedia and I began to look up the political parties in America. I wasn't into politics, but I do know rule number one of being black.

"If thou is Black, thou must be Democrat."

Despite this, I still felt the urge to really understand the different political parties. I looked up the Republican, Libertarian, and Democrat party on Wikipedia. I was surprised to see the beliefs of Republicans. Throughout my life, I don't remember anyone ever saying these things to me. I just always knew that the Republican party was the party of racist white people who only looked out for the rich. They did not care for Black America or Black people in general. They were all wealthy and wanted to stay that way. But when I read about the party on Wikipedia it was a lot different. A lot of what the guy said in the article that they supported made a lot of sense to me.

I also looked at the other parties as well. I went on to do more research on each party's national website. I wanted to see what they have to say about themselves. I dove into articles about each party and their elected officials until I looked up and realized it was 4 o'clock the next morning. I had to decide ASAP.

I don't know why I felt that I had to make a decision that night, but I did. As I stopped and assessed what I had researched, I realized that one party just simply made a little more sense to me. On the other hand, the other party was made up of more people that looked like me. I still had at least another hour debating whether I should go and follow my beliefs or follow the people that looked like me. I ultimately decided to follow my belief system. That belief system is why most of you are reading this book right now. After that moment, I was even more intrigued by politics.

I never really thought much about this world, but I do know that I was a Democrat. When I was in 10th grade we had a Math Teacher named Mrs. Adams. Mrs. Adams was a short lady, no more than 5 feet tall, with blond hair and was sweet as a homemade apple pie. She was fun and funny and while I despised math, I loved Mrs. Adams. During her class we were scheduled to watch a news show that featured teenagers talking about current news and events. On this particular day in 2004, they were having a discussion about President George W. Bush and John Kerry. They showed a clip of President Bush giving an opinion, followed by Senator Kerry.

Mrs. Adams rolled her eyes and scoffed, "*Oh I can't stand that man*". under her breath but we all heard it.

"*You don't like John Kerry?*", one of us asked.

To which she replied, "*Oh God no!*"

"*So, do you like George Bush?*" We asked.

"*Yes. Yes, I do.*" she said.

We immediately started to gang up on her asking questions as to why she could support such a racist man.

"*Don't you like us Mrs. Adams?*"
"*We thought you always liked us?*"
"*But how do you support someone who hates black people?*"
"*How can you support someone who hates poor people?*"
"*Do you hate Black people Mrs. Adams?*"
She looked at each of us and asked, "*Do you really think that I don't like y'all?*"

She seemed hurt by our questions.

"*Well no,*" we answered. "*But you do like George Bush and he don't like Black people.*"

She took off her glasses and said, "*You guys are pretty young and there's a lot about politics and life that you guys will learn as you get older. You'll come to learn that not everything is so black and white. I love all of my students no matter what color you are, and I think you guys know that. Politics has nothing to do with that.*"

She then proceeded with our math lesson for the day. Other than that conversation, I just never really cared about politics, but it was something about this article that struck my interest and made me want to learn more. That summer, I flew through political book after political book. I read books from all sides of the aisle. I wanted to determine if this is really what I believed in. I read books such as *Bamboozled* by Angela McGlowan, *Cooking with Grease* by Donna Brazil, at least three Ann Coulter books and books by the woman that will ultimately become my conservative shero, Condoleezza Rice. I was in love and I was also convinced more than ever that I was a republican. But again, I knew the rules of being black, so I never really shared my views. Well not at first at least.

  At that time, I was working at a black-owned business establishment in the inner city, so naturally most of the other employees were black as well. The presidential election was very heated in 2008. I honestly thought it was because I had just gotten into politics and was just aware of this world on a real-world level, but it really was intense. The intensity was primarily because of the historical implications that this election held. This was the first time in American history where a Black American (Senator back then), Barack Obama, really had a chance to win the presidency. Based on optics alone, his opponent, Senator John McCain, was not nearly as appealing as him. There was so much excitement that election as people really delved into the historical implications of the election and really started to understand the gravity in the way that this election held.

I had made my mind up that I was a Republican was sold on John McCain and I was going to vote for him. It was a normal night. It felt like any other day or else I might have not shown up if I knew it was going to end the way that it did. We had a TV behind the cash register that we turned on when things got slow. The TV was turned on the news of course and Obama was speaking so everyone was fully toned in, holding their breath. After he got done John McCain then came on the screen. As he began speaking everyone turned their backs to the screen, proclaiming that he did not deserve to win the presidency, it was time for change, and how bad he would be for America. I do not know why but I decided to speak up.

"I didn't think that his ideas were that bad."

You could literally hear everyone's necks turn as they looked at me, challenging me to say another word.

"What did you just say?", one of them asked.

"Well I'm just saying that I see that he seems to have some good ideas for the country."

I had done it. I had come out of the closet. But do not worry they beat me back into it. They proceeded to spend the last four hours of our time at work ripping me to shreds. They told me how stupid I was and how I was ignorant of history. They also tried to convince me that I had hated black people and even questioned whether I even wanted it to be black. That was a question I had never thought about. You are just black, or you aren't. At the time I didn't understand that Democrats argue more from the stance of emotion while Republicans argue more from logic. That didn't change the fact that my feelings were hurt by their words. So much so that I went home that night and cried. How could anyone say those kinds of things to me? I did all this research so why don't they do research on both sides as well? All these questions were going through my head and I had nobody to talk to regarding them, but that did not stop me from having my political views and sharing them with my friends.

While their treatment was not as harsh, it wasn't pleasant either. They were adamant that I needed to do more research, look deeper into the racism of the Republican Party, and posed the question of why I should vote for the first black president of the United States of America anyway.

"But what if I don't agree with him on policy?"

That was always my question, and no one could ever answer that. No one ever seemed to care about his policy. They just touted the fact that he talked about hope and change and was a black man. That fall, most of my friends and I grew further and further apart as I was very clear about my policies and they became so ugly about it. I stopped hanging out with them as much because when they had other people around or a crowd, they used the opportunity to diss me and my political views. This ultimately ended in me having long, drawn out conversations that went on for hours with strangers about politics, yet no one could argue with me on policy, which is what I really cared about. I didn't care what elected officials looked like because policy is what's going to be there after that person is no longer in office.

    Before I knew it, it was election day. I went and stood in the super long line to go vote in my first general election. As I waited in line, I heard multiple people talking about how they were so excited to vote for the first black president. There were so many elderly people in the line claiming that they had never voted before but they were not going to miss voting for the first black president. And then it was my turn. I went into the booth to vote but I could not help but stop and second-guess myself on the question of who I wanted to be president. I had to research all the other races as well and voted for all of the Republican candidates to win but I wasn't so sure on the president. After all, this was the first time we will get the opportunity to have a black man hold that office.

    I stood in the ballot box for 5 to 10 minutes. I could not decide! I bet you are holding my breath to see what I ultimately decided to do. I pull the lever for Senator John McCain. No matter what, I just had to vote for the man, and I agreed with more on these things and that to me is what mattered. While working that night I had discovered that Senator Barrack Obama had become the first black president of United States of America. Although I didn't vote for him, I was ecstatic to discover that he had won. This is a good thing for America, and I had hoped that he would bring the change that he had expressed to our nation. After the election, I couldn't help but to want to meet and spend time with people who were like me. I lived in the inner city, so I didn't know anybody like that. I Googled Kansas City Republican and came across a group called the Kansas City Young Republicans. They were having a Christmas party and I was torn about whether this is the best time to come to the party for the first time. I messaged the administrator of the group and asked them if I could attend the party. She said of course, so I mustered enough courage to do so.

A few weeks later I walked into my first ever Republican meeting and I was terrified. So many thoughts ran through my head:

What if they really were racist?
What if they called me out of my name?

Well if they did decide to do that, I figured I would just go back to jail. I went in and timidly asked where they were holding their meeting- The bartender pointed upstairs. Upstairs there were many groups of people, so I went to another bartender and asked him the same question. I literally was whispering to him. As I asked the question for the third time, he shouted, *"Oh you're here for the Republicans. They're right over there!"* I feel so embarrassed. Table of about 15 people turned around and waved for me to come over in a very friendly manner. I went to the table and was greeted by everyone and introduced myself before being seated. They already had plenty of food on the table and they began offering me some of it, as well as seeing what I wanted to drink.

Free food and drinks? Maybe these are my people!

As the night progressed, I got to know everyone in the group and vice-versa. It was a great first introduction to the party. Shortly after they introduced me to something called, Lincoln Days, which was a conference that the state Republican parties held. I got the form and signed up to attend.

There, I was even more nervous than the Kansas City Young Republican meeting. I walked in and there were thousands of people looking at me but hardly any looking *like* me. Naturally, I stood out like a sore thumb. It didn't really bother me as much because I was really interested in just being around anybody that thought the way I did. And boy did they think like me! This meeting allowed me to really get to meet people up close and personal and establish relationship.

They were no different than any of the other people that I had met but we just had the same political philosophy. I am not going to lie, before my years as a Republican, I did spend a lot of time thinking racism or racist comments were lurking around the corner. I couldn't help but to think that eventually something was going to happen because I'm black. After 12 years, it has never happened. Well, except this one time.

    While I wasn't called out of my name, in 2016 a notable Missouri Republican elected official's wife made it pretty clear that she didn't feel that I was welcomed in the party. His comments at events clarified that he stood with her 100%. After truly getting to know people in my party, I do think that they were pretty awesome people. I feel that they just saw me for me. I do think that while most of them would acknowledge that I am of a different skin tone, they were more interested in my political affiliation. I never saw my skin color as a barrier. My experience as a Republican was always centered around finding like-minded people building relationships. And unbeknownst to me, these relationships with help, would help lead me through the hardest time in my life.

Me & My Daughter, Amelia

Chapter 7

Getting married and having children was never part of my life plan. In fact, I never really had much of a life plan. I was more of a *go-with-the-flow* type of girl. While I always liked dating, I never really saw myself having a future with anyone.

Mike was no different. Physically, he fit most of my criteria: handsome, beautiful dark skin, and amazing smile with some of the best teeth I have ever seen in my life. We were never really serious, but it did come at a time where he was the only person that I was seeing. About six months into our *situationship*, I discovered that

I was pregnant. I was devastated. How could this happen to me? I also didn't feel that I was mature enough to really take care of a child. Per the usual, tons of thoughts plagued my mind:

What was going to happen to my dating life?

What about me being able to hang out with my friends?

What about me?

My life was about to be turned upside down at that point and it was all this baby's fault. It was all about to change, and I wasn't happy about it. Being pro-life, abortion wasn't an option and I know my Mother would kill me if I ever gave the baby up for adoption, so I was stuck. My Mother was the first person I had called, and she was ecstatic. She was so excited to become a Grandmother. Even though she had three kids, she didn't really think it was going to happen especially not with me. But here I was. Unwed with a bun in the oven.

Although Mike and I were cool, he wasn't exactly marriage-material, mainly because I never wanted to get married. Even this child wasn't going to change my mind on that. Another thing was bothering me.

As my pregnancy progressed, I couldn't help but think of the situation that I had put her in. I had grown up with no Father in the home and I saw how that affected me. I couldn't believe that I had made choices that will put another person in those same shoes. How could I have been so careless that I had a child without making sure that she had a fully functioning two-parent household? I knew what I had done to her was unfair and then I would have to find some way to fix it.

    I had a very easy pregnancy with no complications. In fact, pregnancy was one of the best things to happen to my body. I was full of energy, only wanted healthy food, and lost over 45 pounds. I felt great. It was actually the healthiest time in my adult life. I reconnected with my love of exercise. I didn't realize how much I missed it and how much my body missed it until I got pregnant and felt really light and energetic. Naturally during pregnancy, I simply did not want any sweets and junk food, so I didn't eat any. My entire pregnancy the only junk food that I ate was some cake at my baby shower. It was delicious but it was just way too sweet for me. She was changing everything about my health.

    The more my pregnancy progressed, the more excited I became. I did things at the beginning because I knew I had to. I talked to her, listened to classical music, and took care of myself but eventually it became because I wanted a healthy baby. As I grew closer to 40 weeks, she still had not turned around my stomach and it seemed like she was going to be breached. The doctor scheduled for me to be induced and the nurse offered to strip my membrane for me just in case. I allowed it and exactly 3 days later, my water had broke. I was shocked at my emotions behind it all. This is something I never want nor envisioned myself doing, yet here I was bringing a life into this world and loving it. My

Mother was so excited that she even came to Kansas City just to witness the birth of her first and only Grandchild. Well a couple of my family members came. My entire family was thrilled to meet Amelia. Most of my cousins had kids yet they still acted like it was something new for them. Along with my family, all my friends, politics and not, were all really excited as well. Everyone's excitement started to annoy me. People calling every single day to check on me. It was nice but got a little irritating after a while.

After 11 and ½ short hours of labor, Amelia Michelle Johnson Conway came into this world. I was able to have a natural birth, which is exactly what I wanted. Labor honestly was not as bad as I thought it would be. She came into this world at 7:42pm on Sunday, October 16th. She was quiet, and just looked around unimpressed. She was yellow and gray, not what I imagined for my newborn. She was not what I expected in size either. I was just under 10 pounds at birth and I just assumed she would be the same. But instead she was born weighing only 7 pounds and 2 ounces, just like her daddy.

After giving birth, everybody left the room and after she was cleaned off, it was just me and Amelia. I talked to her and sang our song. I was in love.

Life with Amelia was simple. She was a quite easy kid and very much a *go-with-the-flow* kind of child. Not a big whiner, which the Lord knew I needed. She was a child that I can take to any kind of function. In fact, I did. She attended numerous political conferences and events with me, and she loved it.

I still couldn't let go of the fact that I had given her the same life that I had which I was not happy about. I told myself that I must re-evaluate my dating life. It was the hardest decision I've ever had to make since I didn't really want to settle down. It was a decision that I wasn't thrilled about, but I knew what I had to do in order to be fair to her. I didn't want her growing up having not ever witness a healthy male-female relationship. Most of the other single mothers I knew didn't hold this as an important thing like I did. In fact, none of them did.

Amelia was a rather good mix of me and her Dad. Fun and outgoing, she also really loved to spend a lot of time alone. Her preschool teacher told me that it was a sign of independence in a child, and that it meant that would not grow up to be a follower. I just felt the need to give her the life that I didn't have, and I didn't mean in the material aspect. I didn't mean just having a Father, but I was very adamant about the areas that I would give her a different quality of life in. Those areas being with her weight and the other, education.

I tried to never feed her fast food. I slipped up only once and was not proud of it. I understood that preparation was key, so I always carved out time for that. She also ate a lot of raw fruits and veggies and so she can develop a love for real whole foods versus processed foods. Despite my efforts, one of her favorite things to eat were chips, which I allowed in moderation of course. I was not going to have her go through the same body issues I struggled with, but it was much more than that. I see so many kids that are heavily obese. Statistic reveal that 1 in every 4 kids has diabetes, which is the first step in a host of other, more deadly, diseases. Most of the black community has high blood pressure among many other areas that we lead in. I also did not want her having an unhealthy relationship with food like I did.

As far as her education, that was *really* my area. By the age of 1, we started homeschooling. Once a day and every day, we would sit down for at least an hour and do schoolwork. She was so accustomed to it that sometimes I would wake up and she would be up already at her desk practicing her writing. She would even grab my notebook if she had no paper and scribble through them practicing. As much as it drove me crazy, I couldn't complain and just went out and bought another one. At age 2, I found a private school that I wanted her to attend called, *Faith Christian Academy*. They were a part-time private and part-time homeschool and I really like that since I do not think women spent enough time with their children in today's society. Now, I just needed to find a career that would allow me the flexibility to homeschool her part time. As I mulled over options, I finally landed on going into real estate. After doing research, I decided that this was a field that I could both be good at and it would allow me the lifestyle that I wanted to live with Amelia. Finally, we were all set!

We always had a good time. We went to a lot of places and I was forced to ride the bus with her. For some reason, I really loved riding the Metro Transportation Bus and meeting people. But our favorite thing to do together was exercise. I would take her to the track, and she loved it. Not just the running around part but she seemed to love organized exercise. So, we did a workout at least four days a week. We ran the track, did stairs, and other little exercises, her favorite one being push-ups. As soon as we would get there, I'd hear, "*See mommy? I'm doing my push-ups!*" My favorite video I have of her is one of her doing push-ups. Her form was terrible, but her enthusiasm was unmatched. I was thrilled to have a child that was excited about exercising.

We were a pretty normal team and I knew I had to create more opportunities for her. One day, an opportunity just fell into my lap. A friend of mine was starting a scholarship program that would help inner-city kids pay for their K-12 private school education. We were visiting her at her house when she asked me if she could use Amelia as her *spokesbaby*. She explained that she would be the first one to go through the program and that she would pay 75% of her private school tuition. Heck yeah! For that she could've practically had her.

She began to lay the foundation for it. It was great to have him help with her school tuition even though it was inexpensive, so I didn't see myself really struggling to afford it even as a single parent. The second opportunity was modeling. A friend of mine owned a modeling and talent agency in Kansas City. We were also friends on Facebook and one day he reached out to me and asked me if I had ever considered entering her into modeling. Of course, the thought had never crossed my mind, but I was game. He asked me to send in some pictures of her and scheduled for us to come in for an interview with the model agency.

I had a habit of explaining things to her even though I was pretty sure she didn't know what was going on, but she learned to just nod her head whenever I was talking, this was no different. Once we got there we had met with the staff and they had interviewed her. I wasn't allowed to talk and when she realized that she didn't mind it because she could talk for days. After the meeting, they told me that they would love to use her to for different gigs that they receive. The only challenge was that there were not many gigs in her age range in the Kansas City market but if any gigs ever would come up, she would be their preferred choice.

While I did not have a positive outlook on motherhood and parenting, I ultimately grew to really love it. I really loved having this child that I was able to influence in a positive way. Although I was constantly in a state of self-progression, I loved the team that I had with her. To me it seemed like there was nothing Amelia and I could not overcome. It is true when people say the love you feel for your child is unexplainable. Unfortunately, I would also experience something else that is unexplainable.

Amelia & Her Father, Michael.

Chapter 8

It was Tuesday, July 14th, 2015. I recall waking up that day feeling like there was absolutely nothing unusual going to happen. Amelia woke me up as usual and went to pick out something to wear for the day. On this day she wanted to wear a dress. I had already picked her clothes out the night before and was adamant that she was going to wear that. I don't know why I didn't just let her wear the dress. She was clearly upset about it and told me in those exact words.

"*Mommy, I'm upset.*"

She was terribly upset as a matter of fact. A little while later, I left for work and said my normal goodbye. I told her that I loved her and gave her a hug. I didn't know it would be the last time I'd see her alive and moving around or I would have never let her go. She left to go with her Father and his girlfriend, which is what she did each day that I had to work. Work that day was normal. It was Taco-Tuesday, so I went to a local restaurant near my job and got my usual three tacos for lunch. As soon as I sat down, I received a call from a number I didn't know. Since a lot of people have my phone number and a lot of the time I am doing something political, I don't know who it ever is that is calling so I make it a habit to answer all calls. It was Mike. He informed me that they were at Children's Mercy Hospital, there had been an accident, and that I needed to come down right away. So, I did.

  I packed up my tacos, told my manager that my child was at Children's Mercy and went down to join them. For some odd reason I didn't think that it would be anything major or serious. A broken arm kept running through my mind. I don't remember being particularly rushed which is odd looking back on it. Once there, I walked to the front desk where two ladies sat. I told them that I had received a call from my daughter's Father and that he had told me that she was in this hospital. They looked up her name in the system and couldn't find her. I stood there waiting as they continued to look for her. I began to grow impatient and blurted out that there had been an accident and that I needed to get up here, so I needed to know the whereabouts of my daughter. They looked at each other and their facial expressions completely changed. It is if something dawned on them.

> "*She must be the one,*" one of them mumbled to the other one.

I didn't even question what she had said, I just followed her to a room down a long hallway.

> "*Just wait in there and they'll be out to speak with you,*" she said.

It didn't even dawn on me that she was looking down the entire time. As soon as I sat down, my phone rang again. It was Clark from the talent agency.

> "*I have great news! We have a gig lined up for Amelia for tomorrow with American Girl!*" He exclaimed.

I told him that I was in the hospital waiting and that Amelia had been admitted. I didn't know what had happened at the time but I told him I would call him back as soon as I found out and I just didn't think that she would be able to make it tomorrow. It seemed like forever sitting in that empty room waiting. Suddenly, the door opened and in walked a slew of doctors and nurses, along with Mike and his girlfriend, Tony. Tony was crying hysterically, and Mike had a look of shock on his face.

> *"I am so sorry Cecilia! I am so, so sorry. I was in an accident. I'm so sorry!"* She cried through tears and snot.

A nurse sat down with her next to me. She told me her name which I don't remember and told me what her position was at the hospital. All I was thinking was where Amelia was. After her introduction she came to tell me that there had been an accident and Amelia was now very sick.

> "*Sick?*" I thought. *"Amelia's not sick. She was just fine this morning."*

She then told me that she had been run over by a car.

> "*Oh, you mean hit by a car*", I interrupted.

> "*No, she was run over by a car and she is currently in critical condition. We have her sedated so she doesn't feel any pain and we have to run CAT scans to make sure she can recover from this.*", she explained.

My brain was still stuck on the "*run over by a car.*" How does one get run over by a car? She continued to speak.

> *"We're doing everything we can to make sure that she makes a full-recovery, but you must understand that your daughter is really, really sick."*

It was then that I noticed a chaplain in the room. As soon as I looked at him, she told me his name and that he was the hospital chaplain. He was there to help families cope with their situation.

> *"What situation? Where is my daughter?"*, I asked while standing up.
>
> *"I want to see my daughter. Where is she?"*

She said we are going to go back to see her but repeated that she was very sick. We left a room and I followed her down what had seemed like the longest hallway I've ever seen in my life. As we reached the end of it she said, *"Take a right, right here."* I made a right and kept walking. She gently grabbed my arm and said, *"No. She's right here."* I looked up and there was a small room with a few sliding, glass doors. In the room there stood about 25 doctors and nurses. And then I saw it. Amelia's left foot. As soon as I saw it, they all looked up at me. They begin to park like the Red-Sea, and I saw her lying there. I slowly walked towards her trying to make sure that this was really her. It was. She lied there completely motionless with tubes in her nose. Her mouth and stomach protruding out as if she were pregnant. I could not believe what I was seeing. As soon as I got to her side, she flatlined. All of the doctors immediately went into motion. They started to try and resuscitate her. One of the nurses grabbed my hand, placed it on her leg and told me to talk to her.

I was too scared to speak, she just felt different. I placed my hand back on her leg. I had no words, so I started to sing her song. From the moment Mike and I had decided on her name, I would sing the chorus of the song *Cecilia* by Simon and Garfunkel, but I had put Amelia in the place of Cecilia. I always sang it to her as she fell asleep in my arms and each time she had hurt herself.

> "*Amelia you're breaking my heart. You're shaking my confidence daily. Oh Amelia, I'm down on my knees. I'm begging you please come home now. Come on home.*"

A few seconds later, the machines started beeping again letting me know that she was back. I stood there looking at her and my baby didn't look like my baby anymore. Sure, she still looked the same, but something was off. She was never this still. After she came back, the surgeon pulled me aside. He informed me that she was going to need emergency surgery to stop the internal bleeding. He informed me that she was also going to need a liver because her liver had been crushed and that she was going to be placed on the list to receive one.

"*What are her chances of surviving?*", I asked.

"Well miss we're going to do everything we can to help her and she's just really sick" he replied.

"That's not what I asked you. But I get it. I understand. I see all these doctors and nurses here, so I know it's not good. I promise you. I am not going to tear this place apart. I'm not going to set it on fire. I am a realist so please be real with me. What are my chances of walking out of here with my daughter alive?'

I was pleading at this point. He looked around, took a step closer to me and said, *"There really is no chance."* I completely zoned out. At that moment I accepted that she was never going to be with me again but honestly, I knew that from the moment I saw her laying in a hospital bed. I didn't really see her making it. At that moment Mike came over and tried to tell me that he was sorry. He tried to hug me which pissed me off. I started to swing throwing punches his way. The doctors and nurses pulled me off of him and ushered me into a small room with a friend who had joined me at the hospital. I made a Facebook status stating that she had been in an accident and to pray for her. I wasn't ready to tell the world what I knew, and I was just too heartbroken just thinking about the word. I knew prayer wasn't going to change anything about the situation. I knew my baby was gone. As my friends and family saw the status, they began to reach out to me. I communicated with a few of them exactly what was going on, but I only told two of them what the real situation was, Britney and Jan. I knew there was no way around this. Even when I'm going through the worst thing ever, I was still thinking about protecting everybody else and their feelings. I didn't know if they could stomach hearing those words just yet.

A few minutes later the surgeon came to the room. He informed me that they were able to stop the internal bleeding but then she was still really sick, and they were doing everything they could to help make her well. He rambled on but his words weren't processing in my brain Almost immediately a nurse burst into the room and said we're losing her again.

I rushed back into the room where she was. And sure enough, her machine was buzzing letting me know that she was flatlining again. I went over to her side and grabbed her arm in my hand.

> *Please don't do this to me, Amelia baby. Please don't leave me. I need you just wake up so we can go and play.*

I looked up and the nurse was performing CPR. I don't remember much about it except remembering thinking that she was pretty. She had blonde hair and the bluest eyes. Those eyes filled with tears more and more as time went by. She wasn't saying anything, but her eyes just kept apologizing to me. It's like tears started to come down her face and neither one of us could break the trance that we were in.

The doctor then came, put her hand on my shoulder and informed me that they have done all that they can do. Turns out this was the third time losing her in 3 and ½ hours. I couldn't believe it. All I could do is cry. I also started to talk to her saying the first thing that came to my brain:

> "*I can't believe that I'm having to say goodbye to you, but I am. Whatever you do, don't be scared. Don't be scared. There's going to be a light and you just walk into it. There's also going be a man. Just take his hand and go with him. Don't look back, just go with him. Where you are going is the perfect place. You're going to have so much fun. You get to meet your Uncle, your Grandfather, and a lot of other people when you get there. Don't worry about me because one day I'm going to be up there too. Just have fun and enjoy yourself and remember so many people love you but nobody as much as me.*"

I cry every time I recall the event of having to say those words to her. I informed everyone what had happened. Friends and family had already started showing up at the hospital. They wanted to show their support for her and me as well and to say their goodbyes. Nobody believed what they saw. Everyone just stood there quietly crying to themselves. I don't even remember who all came because I was so fixated on the site in that hospital bed. The nurse came in and cleaned her up and asked me if I wanted to hold her. Of course, I wanted to hold her. Her body felt so much heavier than it ever felt. I held her as long as I could. I held her for about 45 minutes until my arm felt like they would fall off. There I sat in that rocking chair looking down at her, crying.

While I know it was not her decision to go, I still couldn't wonder why she left me. About an hour later someone came in and informed me that the coroner was there. They told me that they will stay as long as I could so I can have as much time with her as possible. I asked everyone else to leave the room so I could just spend my time with her alone. Once alone, I closed the curtains so that we could have privacy. I climbed in the bed with her and held her like I've done for the last almost 4 years.

> "We had such a good run. When I got pregnant with you, I didn't think that it would be this much fun. You brought so much joy to my life. You gave me so much direction with a sense of being that I don't think I would've gone without you."

I continued to talk to her non-stop saying everything that came to my mind until I received the message that the coroner absolutely had to leave. He came in and they covered her body with a white sheet and carried her out. I just stood there watching, wishing she would make just a slightest movement and wake up. But it was decided. She was gone and I was alone.

As I walked with one of my friends to their car another friend had informed me that there was media there and they wanted to see if I would speak to them. The accident was running in every media outlet. There was also a text message sent out to multiple people regarding an accident, but they had no idea that it was Amelia. My friend told me that I didn't have to talk to them which I already knew but I agreed to do the interview. As I answered their questions, I couldn't help but notice that they were all in tears. After the interview they came out to me one by one expressing their sorrow and informed me that they had children as well and I couldn't imagine what I was going through and that they prayed for my healing. It was the most positive experience I've ever had with the media actually.

    My car was parked on the other side of the hospital, so I went through the hospital to get to it. Friends of mine were sitting in a waiting area. I thought everyone had left. I walked up to them and they hugged me and told me they were sorry. I joined them and we all sat in silence, crying.

> "*I cannot believe that I'm leaving this hospital without her with me. I never thought something like this would happen to me,*" I cried.

After about an hour I told them I was going home but I couldn't go home. I got in my car and looked at my rearview mirror. Her car seat was still there. I began crying and controllably. Afterwards, I just went over to a friend's house and spent the night. Over the next weeks I would just stay at people's houses because I couldn't sleep at home.

The next day I woke up wishing it were a dream. I knew that it wasn't. This is my first time in over three years waking up without my child there to bug me for a banana or some strawberries. I honestly don't know what was worse: witnessing what I saw in the hospital room or waking up childless.

Next came the funeral plans. She was so young that I've never even considered having life insurance. Nobody thinks that their child is going to die at such a young age. I didn't have enough money to cover the funeral expenses but a friend of mine reached out offering to help pay for the funeral. As I got on my Facebook that morning, I noticed that there was a GoFundMe link at the top of my newsfeed. The GoFundMe page was for me!

Two of my friends who didn't know each other had set up two separate accounts in order to help me pay for the funeral expenses. I was so fortunate for the friends in my life. Thanks to my girlfriends, Avia and Rachel, not having enough money was not a problem that I had to concern myself with. After two days, I received a message from a friend referring me to the funeral home and I reached out to them to start the plans. I called my Pastor and spoke with him about using the church to host the funeral. I knew there would be a lot of people there because she had met a lot of people due to our large families, traveling, and politics.

Nobody wants to plan to bury their child. So, I chose not to. My Dad had died a year before and he was cremated. His wife had provided me and each of my siblings with heart shaped urns filled with his ashes so that we can each have a piece of him, so I decided to do the same thing with Amelia. I also wanted to do something else that was non-traditional. Instead of having a funeral, we would have a Home Going Celebration. I would make this the most joyous occasion that I possibly could. I also set a particular dress code.

Everyone wanted to dress in the essence of Amelia. Dressing like a cartoon character, princess, or fairy was the requirement. I would be her favorite character of all, Minnie Mouse. Thanks to the Go Fund Me accounts, I was also able to assist my family with travel arrangements for her to come up and to attend the funeral.

On Friday, July 24th, over 450 people attended the funeral of my daughter. To my amazement everyone's attire really cheered me up. There were so many festive looking people that I couldn't help but feel warm on the inside. Everyone really did just as I asked. Not a piece of black in sight. People came dressed as characters from popular Disney movies, they wore T-shirts with cartoon characters, tiaras, and fancy dresses. Some of them even made T-shirts with Amelia's picture on it, it was a sight to see. I remember seeing my friend Becky dress up like the American flag. Amelia loved the American flag. It was something that started as a joke where I taught her facts about the flag. And as we progressed, she would. When we attended political events, she would always go up to someone, tug on their pant and teach them facts about the American flag.

"That's the American Flag."
"It has 13 stripes and 50 stars."
"The 13 stripes represent the 13 colonies."
"The 50 stars represent the 50 states."
"It's red, white, and blue."

People would look down at her and couldn't help but to laugh at his toddler trying to teach them facts about the flag. It was very cute, nonetheless.

At her funeral, we enjoyed prayers, songs, and of course the Pledge of Allegiance. Amelia wouldn't have it any other way. And then it was my turn to speak. I don't remember anything I said but I do remember feeling the love and support in that. Everyone was so amazing. I couldn't help but feel the love. It felt like she was still there, but I knew she wasn't.

Life after Amelia has been 1,000,000% different. No matter where I'm at, I have to cope with seeing everyone else's children continue to grow up and experience the things that my child never got the chance to experience. Even five years later, there is still so many triggers that I have. Some of them are still uncontrollable. It's still difficult for me to walk past children's clothes in stores. That's actually one of the hardest things to do. It took a while for me to feel, I guess, normal again if that is even a word I can use. I know that no matter what my life will never be normal. As much as I try and want to, I can never go back to the life I lived with her.

She impacted me for the better in so many ways. She made me so much better as a person. With her, I actually had goals and plans that I had lined up for us to do. While it's usually the parents that offer structure, she actually brought so much into my life and I thank her for that. She was everything I didn't know that I needed. As much as I would love to have her still here with me, I am thankful to have had that experience with her, I really am. There is not a day that by that I don't think about her. There is not a day that I do not have a memory of her. It took me two years to stop crying every day, I still cry a couple times a week about her. This is my life and I accepted it but given the chance to do it over again, I would.

My heart and soul feel empty a lot of times. The longing for her is the worst. Not having her near me and knowing that I never can is painful. But there is a lot of solace in knowing that one day I will see her, and we will be together again. I really longed for the day that I can see her again and have her run into my arms and to be called mommy again.

Me & Dr. Ben Carson

Chapter 9

Like most things in my life, Amelia changed my political views. Well, maybe change is not the best word to use. She more like offered more focus in my political career. Before and during her life I was kind of going with the flow as usual. I have worked a lot of different jobs in the political arena for organizations, campaigns, and even a pregnancy resource center. I really was just taking any opportunity that came at me for the most part, but I loved it, nonetheless. It was not until her that I really started to zone in on what I really wanted to do politically. I don't have a college degree so there were a lot of things that I wasn't necessarily qualified for but that didn't stop me from still getting those positions. My passion for politics and power was undeniable to anyone that met me. That is the real reason I think I was able to be successful and climb the ladder in my own right.

It is a very unique position to be in being a young black female who is also Republican in America. You are a unicorn which, if you look at statistics, I completely understand but that does not explain the way people treat you. Throughout the years I have faced my fair share of challenges within my race due to my political beliefs. Now, I do think I have reached the point to where most people understand me and are more open minded that has not always been the case. I have been in situations where people have tried to fight, jump me, and spit at me all because I identify as a Republican. As a young black conservative, you do often feel alone at times. Sure there are other black conservatives but they tend to be in a different age group and you never really have anyone that's your age to discuss these kinds of things, share your views, and dig deeper into those views. In 2018, I was invited to the White House while attending a summit in Washington DC. Over 450 young black Americans from all walks of life attended as well.

The East Wing of the White House was filled with us walking around and exploring our house all while representing in our MAGA gear to celebrate and show our support for the sitting president, Donald Trump. While the media has done a lot to portray President Trump in a certain light, that didn't stop Black people from coming out and supporting him more than they've supported any Republican presidential candidate in recent history. The media, including black media, used this time instead of trying to gain an understanding of why we believe what we believe but instead to show us in a negative light. This was especially the case for black media. According to them we were all given MAGA hats at the White House and we were all issued checks from the Trump campaign for coming out.

> *On a side note: Next time I see President Trump, remind me to ask him where my check is because I sure did not get it.*

They cannot accept the fact that Black people were waking up and choosing to take a good hard look at politics from a different perspective and make decisions based off of that. Honestly, a part of me thinks they do which is why they must hammer so hard at the racist narrative that they push so feverishly.

They are witnessing this with their own, but they cannot let other black Americans see this. Hence why our media never wants to talk about it and why every black conservative or Republican is still identified as sellouts, coons, or Uncle Toms- That's Aunt Tommineisha to you!

It seems like even if the conservative platform could help better our community, they do not want to do it just because it is coming from the right. As a black conservative you are put in a unique box of your own by both your race and your party. While most people of your race regurgitate these names and see you as someone who doesn't care about your community, they're sometimes second-guessing their names with conservatives themselves, especially regarding your political beliefs and your allegiance to your political beliefs versus your race. It is like everybody wants you to choose their side, but I've made it clear that I'm choosing both sides. Both the black community and conservative community don't understand how much they have in common. They both hold the same philosophies and get in their own way unbeknownst to themselves.

I have a theory, but I do not quite know what to call it yet. This theory displays what I just laid out: that the black and conservative community have a lot of commonalities in their behavior and that makes it that much harder for them to progress. Being a member of both communities, you get to take a step back and witness this and it really does make a lot of sense although, I am sure these two parties may disagree.

For starters, external versus internal issues are priority subjects to discuss. Both communities have a habit of looking at their external problems versus looking at the internal things, which could be the catalyst for change. In the black community you hear a lot about racism, the man, and the system and I am not saying that they are not true. Instead of focusing on things that are internal things that they can change, they choose to point the finger at everything that is outside of them. It is easy to sit here and point at White America and that systematic racism as your main problem but what about the problems that you create for yourselves? What about the barriers we create that become hurdles for us and our children?

I had a child out of wedlock and to this day over 75% of black children are also birthed from the same situation, out of wedlock. This not only compromises the Mother's mental health but also the children as well. Black women are being forced to raise children alone because whether it's the Father or the Mother's fault, nobody's making a decision to really build a strong relationship and get married before bringing children into this world and our children are the ones that are suffering the most. Of course our children are going to be trapped in failing schools because they have a single one that, like my Mother, had multiple children so no she more than likely can't afford private school or to move into a better community that offers a better education for her children. It does not mean she does not care but it is just the reality of her situation. So we can't continue to ignore the barriers and hurdles we put before ourselves and instead ask someone else to change their behavior when we have a lot of things that we can work on to change our behavior as well. By not truly addressing these things, we never really absorb the full impact and disservice that we place on our amazing Women and underserved children.

The conservative community is no different. We love to sit around and talk about how the media is brainwashing people, the Democrat party is lying to the black community, how black immunity can't see past those lies, and how the Democrat party on the left is painting the Republicans in a certain way. We never seem to realize that nobody is stopping *us* from going into the black community and explaining things from our point of view. We get upset because underserved communities are not given the tools to succeed yet when are *we* going to try to share that with them? We claim our platform offers better ways to pull yourself up by your bootstrap but why are we not putting actions behind that word to prove that? There is an old saying that goes '*Actions speak louder than words.*" Where is the action? You can tell me all day that the Democrats and the left are lying to me but at least they are in my community offering a helping hand. When will we be the party that looks out for the little guy?

    We have a bevy of resources at our fingertips now, so when was the last time we tried to offer those resources to the Black community? For example, we talk about entrepreneurship being the American dream; We talk about how it can lift any American out of poverty. So, what is stopping us from going into the inner city setting up an urban co-working space offering people the space and resources to start their small businesses? We have a lot of successful business owners on our side so why not have those guys offer wisdom to help guide the small business owners in different areas such as marketing, branding, and accounting? Help does not have to look the way you are used to seeing it look. Showing someone what you mean is far more effective than telling them; Yet, both groups would rather sit around and complain about what someone else is doing instead of saying let me control what I can control.

Both groups are also very guilty of short-term thinking. If you look at a lot of things that the left has accomplished in America none of it happened overnight. Whether it is abortion, gay marriage, or getting the Bible out of schools, those things did not happen overnight. In fact, the people who started on those missions and down those pathways did not live to see it come to fruition. Long-term thinking is a must if you want to get any real change in America. I am not here to argue whether I agree or disagree with rioting or tearing down statues, but I *am* here to argue that those things offer no long-term solutions. If you're thinking in terms of longevity and we want something to be changed, there has to be a plan in order to get it to change and that plan does not always include people being on their soapbox telling other people how they should just do this and be in there wrong about that.

Perhaps the biggest issue that I see with both groups is the fact that they do not educate children. Almost a year before his death, Malcolm X famously quoted, *"Only a fool will let his enemy educate his children."* Both conservatives in the black community have expressed their dissatisfaction with the public-school system, neither of whom oversee it. Black people acknowledge that we are not taught our history in inner-city public schools or anything for that matter. We are not taught the basic skills that we need to succeed in America in predominantly black public schools. Conservatives complain about liberal indoctrination in schools at every meeting or summit that I attend. They complain that their sexuality is being forced on their children's throats yet neither group makes the effort to take their children's education into their own hands. The exception to this is that an overwhelming majority of black and conservative children make up a great deal of the American public education system. Instead of complaining that there is no prayer in school, why not open the doors of our churches? So many churches sit empty throughout the week when we could be using them to educate our children and this will allow us to determine was is being learned and taught.

If you want your children to learn a more African-based education why not do it yourselves? It is perfectly legal to start a private school in America so why continue to complain about the lack of quality education or the things that their children are receiving in their public schools when you could do something about it. We constantly want someone that we have identified as our enemy to provide a better service to us and our children. Both of us are guilty of this.

Anytime I go to a community meeting or go to a conservative meeting the same thing Is being said by the person holding the microphone, yet no one realizes that they can change this. Either they do not realize it, or they just do not want to do the work and are okay with just complaining about it. I do not know which one is the truth. I just know that I do not know either one gets us to where we want to be. Our kids continue to suffer as I did in my failing inner-city public schools.

I recently looked up the proficiency rates from the last testing at my alma mater. To my surprise, I discovered that only 12% of the students were proficient in English. No students were on grade level for math. Does this mean that those students are stupid, dumb, or mindless? Absolutely not! It means that they are not being given a fair chance at a quality education and it is only going to get worse; it always has. So, why continue to allow these brilliant minds that are filled with so much potential continue to waste away?

Now, I do understand that there are certain circumstances- such as single-parent households and low-income households- that prevent people from being able to afford a private education and to some extent that is true. But at some point we do have to make our children's education a priority over the things that we buy and the money that we spend on things such as birthday parties, clothes, shoes, toys, and iPhones. It all boils down to what you care about and to determine that, simply look at what you spend your money on. This is not necessarily a soapbox moment, but I would really like to leave you with those thoughts of what is most important to me.

I honestly believe that Americans are in control of their own destiny. There have been times in American history where my people have not always had this privilege. From slavery, to Jim Crow to not having the ability to vote for people that represent them, we have not always had it easy. America has come a long way in those efforts. That does that mean that we have a long way to go. absolutely not! But we are fortunate to live in a time where we do have a lot more control and say-so over our lives. I acknowledge that I could have been more successful in my life and I could have been more focused and more serious about pressing issues. But the beautiful thing is that we are getting better with each generation. That is why it is imperative that we make sure that the next generation has a fair chance whether you are Black, White, or Hispanic. Our kids deserve a quality education. But most are not receiving it in American public-school system and that is not fair. The left promises to throw more money at if that solves the problem but does it ever really?

    I just want us as Americans to realize our potential. It is embedded in our DNA; We can take our country back. We do not have to accept what we have been given. We do not have to accept what others think we should be given. Our history is so rich. There are so many exceptional people all over our country that want change and we can make it happen, collectively.

Me & President Donald J. Trump

Chapter 10

Throughout my 32 years on this earth, I've been through a lot. In fact, you just read the bulk of it. A lot of my readers have known me for a long time, yet you never knew the extent of half of my traumatic experiences. There are very few people prior to me writing this who even knew things that happened in my life. One of my closest friends recently asked me after revealing to her the number of encounters with sexual assault, "*Why don't you ever talk about this stuff? I would've never known this about you.*"

The truth of the matter is I do not want my entire life's existence to be centered around my pain and traumatic experiences. There is so much more to me that I would like to be highlighted . So, I share these experiences now. Why now? Honestly, it was not my intention to talk about all these things when I set out to write this book. I intended on writing an entirely political book that was sprinkled with a few memories of my upbringing. Once I decided this was a memoir, I knew that it would have to be much deeper than just a political read. After all of that, I am more than just my politics. Just as I am more than my pain, traumatic experiences, and occurrences of abuse. Although I have been through all these things, I never really looked at myself as someone who has had a "*hard life.*"
    I witness people all the time who use their pain in their background as a tool for one-upping the next person. Everybody wants to be the victim; Everybody wants to be scorned; Everybody wants everybody to know what has happened to them. And to me- for the most part- it is not genuine, that is not me. I do not believe in running around with my pain on my sleeve. Yes, I have been through all these things and yes, I have had some after-effects that I have had to work through. Does that mean that my entire present and future must be centered around those things? Absolutely not!
    Most people look at me and even though they know me, they still find a hard time believing that I have been through these experiences. Not that I do not believe me having such a tough exterior has nothing to

do with that. It is hard to fathom a person like me going through so much in just 32 years of life, but I have. But I want to make this clear and say it loud enough for everybody to hear.

I Am Nobody's Victim.

I choose to hold the philosophy that no matter how many times life knocks you down, that only gives you more opportunities to get back up. No matter what I go through life will never get the best of me. And this is just that – a choice. It is not an easy choice to make but it is a choice. I have spent so much time not really facing the aftermath of some of the things that have happened to me, mainly the sexual abuse. Instead, I chose to bury it in the back of my head for the most part. I have seen the outcome of that, and I now understand the need to work through these things. Whether it be therapy, self-reflection, or through Religion, choose to work on the thoughts that trigger pain and negativity. I chose all three. I could not have gone through these things had I not, especially without Jesus. When I finally saw what I was doing to myself, I had to be honest with myself and acknowledge that I needed him to help see me through this; To help guide me through this.

    Sometimes when you are in the mist of trauma, it is hard to believe that there is a pot of gold at the end, but it is there. I have reclaimed my pot of gold. I know it is not a physical pot, although I wish it were. My pot of gold is in my future. I have chosen to let my future be my prize. There's so much power in there. So much power in working towards what will become. So much power in seeing who you are and enjoying the journey. So much power in meeting each version of you as you get to that journey. There is just so much more. And I have not even scratched the surface of my future. I've been involved in politics for about 12 years now. All my political experiences have been on the local and state level. I have thoroughly enjoyed my political journey. I know that it is just the beginning.

A little over a year ago I received a call from President Trump's re-election camp. They had reached out to me via text a few days before, but I thought it was just another one of those text messages that I signed up for to help with this campaign. As it turned out, I had been recommended to them to be a part of Trump's campaign. I was truly shocked. I have not done anything on *that* magnitude that would justify them calling me in my opinion. I have only been active in Missouri, and all my social media numbers were not exactly stellar. But I was not about to bring that up. After my vetting, they invited me to be a member of the advisory board as a member of Black Voices for Trump. It was a new coalition geared towards working to garner more votes for the President of the 2020 election and to also get President Trump's *real* message out. Even my friends and family who cannot stand President Trump were excited for me. Here I was being given the opportunity to do exactly what I have been wanting the Republican Party to do since becoming a Republican, reaching out to more black voters. I was so extremely excited to be able to be a part of the coalition. It has been nothing short of amazing. I have been able to travel, meet great people and really fine-tune my belief system.

In 2016 when most conservatives I knew were running around panicking about what the outcome to the election would be, I remained very calm. I already knew, President Trump. When people ask me how I know this and why I seemed so sure, the answer was always the same. I have never had so many Black people approach me and tell me that they were voting for a Republican candidate. What is more shocking is, I have never seen so many on a national level so excited to do so. At a certain point I was in disbelief. After all, the media was doing a number on him painting him as the most racist person ever born on the face of the planet and it seemed to be working even to me. While he was not my first pick, after Rick Perry had gotten out of the race, I hopped on the Trump train.

Even with the media, Hollywood, and many times his own party against him, President Trump won the election in November of 2016. I was quite sure that he'd come in swinging, but I didn't know that he'd knock many people out.

After his release of the New Black Deal to Media Take Out, my support for him only grew. It skyrocketed as soon as he started to deliver all those things that he promised. For the first time in a long time we have someone who not only set an agenda to address many of the things that we have highlighted as issues we faced in our community but he actually worked to execute it. From his stance on school choice, to his support of HBCUs, to his signing of true criminal justice reform, we finally have a president that is listening to us. A president that has really put forth an effort to show that he is a President for all Americans ,not just the majority. So many choose to only focus on his words that have been sliced and diced by the media before it is even delivered to you, I like to focus on his actions, his policies. For that is the one thing that is going to remain once he is out of office after his second term.

As I previously stated, for most of my political career I have been sort of wandering around aimlessly. With everything that has occurred, my path is only becoming clearer. Well, I have never been one to really like children, I have found this great need to help them. Our children deserve better than what we have given in the past and are giving out in the present. Children are the Nation; They are the future.

(Insert Whitney Houston singing, "*The Greatest Love of All*").

I really feel the need to be in the fight for education equality. Children in America of all walks of life deserve to see a quality education. I want to make sure that I can help as many kids get there as possible. I started this final chapter off talking about my optimism for my future and what does it hold? To answer that, it holds a lot of things that I cannot even see yet. When I first came out as a supporter of President Trump, people often asked me a question that used to really stop me in my tracks. When was America ever great? I would go over this question a lot as I desperately wanted to answer it. Now, let's be clear- I KNOW America is great.

The challenge was coming up with the wording that would bury that question every time I answered it. As I worked through this it, like most things, the subject became about me. One day I was talking to my Mother about it. Now Mother is not particularly into politics, but we were discussing *Make America Great Again*. Then I said, "*What makes Cecilia great?*" It did not take long for me to answer that.

Cecilia was great when she overcame not only low self-esteem but her desire for ending her life and chose to overcome instead of giving in; She was great when she chose to forgive her Father after a lifetime of broken promises and heartbreak; She was great when she dealt with the aftermath of having her innocence stolen from her as a child and overcoming it once again as an adult; She was great when she chose to judge political leaders and elected officials not by the color of their skin but by how their policies could better affect her community and all of America; She was great when she decided not to let people break her with hurtful words because of how she chose to vote; She was great when she decided to pen her first book and decided to pour not only her heart and soul into it, but her pain as well in the hopes of helping other people.

You see, America is not unlike any individual. It is made great by how it overcomes obstacles; It was made great when it is knocked down, but it gets back up for another round; It is made great when it realizes it's short-coming and wrong-doings; It is made great when Americans realize a problem, inequity, and injustice and fight to change it. I do not think there is a person dead or alive that will not say that this nation isn't perfect and faces a different set of challenges. Every nation has, but what makes America great is our founding doctrines that lay out the guidelines for our nation. No, it has not been an easy ride but that is a part of the beauty of us. Most nations do not have this kind of foundation and that is what made us a leader- The *idea* of America.

    See, I am no different than you. I am human and I make mistakes. Things have happened that have been out of my control. Things of happened to me that have been because of me. But can I really call myself great if I do not learn from that and come out of it as a better person? This is something that we must all decipher for ourselves. No matter what you decide, just make sure you decide to be great.

Me & My Mother | Emma Johnson

Dedications

Well, first and foremost above anything, I would like to thank Jesus Christ, my Lord and Savior. Thank you for the person that I am and instilling the characteristics that I have. You have truly saved my soul.

I must thank my Mother above any other human being. She truly is the most amazing woman that I know. If I am lucky, I will be $1/10^{th}$ of the woman that she is. Caring, sweet, intelligent, she is all the things that I aspire to be. Calling my Mother an angel is a great understatement. She does not know how much I have done for her. She has done for me my whole life and I look forward to paying those favors to her. The greatest of these gifts being displaying a good example of a role model. I absolutely have the best Mother.

I absolutely must thank my one and only daughter, Amelia. You came as swiftly as you left, and I am thankful for both experiences. Thanks to you, I know what unconditional love is. I promise you that I will make you proud and I will make sure that you get the legacy that you deserve. I only had you for four years, and you will live in my heart until the day I die. I look forward to the day that I will get to see you again, embrace you again, and experience you again. For that, I cannot wait.

There are so many people that have had a tremendous impact in my life so I do not know how much more dedications I can give, but I will list some of the most-impactful ones

First, I would like to thank my family, all my aunts, uncles, and cousins. You guys are my true motivators. Auntie Bernadette, Auntie Dolly, Uncle James, Uncle Willie, Uncle Curly, Uncle Hosie, and the late great Uncle Leroy- Thank you guys for more than you will ever know.

To my younger siblings, DJ and Jalissa, your looking up to me really motivates me to keep moving forward. This is perhaps one of the greatest things that pushes me- Knowing that you are always looking to me for guidance and direction and I hope to always be able to offer it. Rest in heaven, Trevor Orlando Johnson.

To my cousins, Ashley, Marcus, Tremelle, Dee, Dante, Dan, Trey, Tiara, Nana, Rell, Christina, Trevon, Trevelle, Jelly, Jamion, JaCorey, and the late great DeLo- Thank you for being my extended siblings. Growing up with you guys has really shaped and molded me into many ways. We are all on our own paths, yet we all continue to come together to have each other's back and help each other out and I hope we stay that way. By the way, you were all so lucky for given the chance to grow up with me.

To my Grandmother, Lucille: While you may not realize it, you are such a tremendous force to be reckoned with. Your short and witty form of love has affected me in great ways. I do not expect the same kind of love from every person I encounter but I do appreciate it. I admire you so much Grandma. You are such an inspiration for me, and I love you so dearly. Your life is living proof that we can overcome no matter what we face and what we must endure. Your strength has left a great mark on me.

To my closest inner circle of friends - My Buddy, Avia, Cierra, Britney W., Brittany M., Britney W, Alex, Natalie, Brian, Lisa, Jan, Shannon, Jalissa, and the best of them all – Ernestine, thank you all for choosing to be my extended family. While we don't talk all the time, whenever we do it is if we never took a break. While you were all close friends of mine most of you have never crossed paths and probably never will. That is simply because each of you play a key role in different areas of my life. You and I know those roles so there's no need to list them on here. Nobody brings me joy like you guys. You have been there for me through my many trials and tribulations especially through the hardest days of my life. Y'all may get on my nerves, but I would not change any of that for the world. Okay, maybe I will trade you in for a rich man but y'all knew that.

To Shanteai, thank you for forcing me to be as open as I was here. You have one of the biggest hearts I have ever encountered. We may not see eye to eye at times and you can be a bit intense, I truly value your views and thoughts. May you become what you aspire to be and more. You deserve the world and you will get it.

And to you- The person reading book: You have explored the deepest and darkest corners of my life. Thank you for giving me your time.

-Cecilia S. Johnson-

MEET THE AUTHOR

In a life filled with meaning and accomplishment, Cecilia S. Johnson has emerged as one of the conservative movement's most compelling young figures. As the founder of multiple urban organizations, she has helped create an environment in Missouri where minority voices and issues are heard prompting real solutions. Originally from a small trailer park in Southeast Arkansas, her Mother announced she was moving her and her little sister to the East Side of Kansas City, Missouri. Unwilling to relocate, she tried everything she could to keep her Mother from moving to such a violent area where she would surely be robbed and shot like they showed on TV.

In 1997, she moved to the city and quickly adapted to the faster pace of life there. She spent the remainder of her childhood and teenage years in various failing inner-city public schools. In 2006, she graduated from Central Greek Classical Academy, at the time labelled one of the worst performing schools in the state of Missouri.

In April 2008, while waiting for a friend to receive her prescription at a local Walgreens, she decided to flip through some magazines and came across an article by a black man explaining why he was a Republican. Confused, she read the article and found herself agreeing with his reasonings. Not only was he black, but he also came from a single parent inner-city background which she really related to. That night she researched the political parties on online and decided that she would become a Republican. Still a freshman in college, she dropped out of college already annoyed with the very blatant liberal bias her professors not only held but tried to shove down their students' throats.

In 2012, she took her first political position as a Volunteer Coordinator for Americans for Prosperity. Soon after, she started consulting on campaigns and giving speeches on her experience in the Republican Party and how we can attract more black people to the party. In 2013, while working as the Urban Outreach Coordinator for Rachel House Pregnancy Resource Center, she founded her own organization called Hood Conservatives (now The Right Direction). Hood Cons actively engaged the black community by displaying conservative ideas such as lower taxes, entrepreneurship, and school choice.

On July 14, 2015, her world changed forever. While at work, her 3-year-old daughter Amelia was accidentally run over by a car. Less than 4 hours later after emergency surgery, Amelia stopped breathing for the third time and was pronounced dead. One month later, Cecilia accepted a position running the Lt Gov. campaign for Bev Randles. Throwing herself into work, she traveled the state of Missouri meeting voters and working to make history in hopes of getting the first black statewide office holder in the state. Falling a little short that August, she continued to consult and work for local campaigns. In December 2016, she took a position as a car salesman at a certified Nissan dealership, ultimately becoming the Owner Loyalty Manager. Today you can find her giving speeches across the country and working to further the Conservative Movement in the black community. She is the former and the first Black President of the Kansas City Young Republicans and is the first black office holder of the Missouri Federation of Young Republicans. In 2012, she was awarded as Red Alert Politics 30 under 30, celebrating 30 young conservatives under the age of 30 working to advance the conservative movement. In 2019, she was selected to be an advisory board member for Black Voices for Trump Coalition.

The Right Direction

Our right-of-center dedicated "The Right Direction" to all of the advocates who work hard to keep our nation going forward in the right direction by helping non-traditional conservative candidates succeed in their quest for bettering our nation. We are also aiding various communities all over America by helping to build up their existing organizations, businesses, and brands.

On the following pages, you will meet conservative activists and brands that are on the ground putting forth the efforts to ensure that the conservative message is received throughout the country to ALL Americans.

Amelia & The Lil Patriots- Coming Soon!

Amelia is your average little girl. Thanks to the values instilled by her parents, she loves everything about America. Her Father is a U.S. History Professor at a local university. Every night after dinner, they bond while watching his lectures from that day. On her 5th birthday, he presents her with a special gift, a pocket-watch that allows her to travel back in time and witness any historical event! The next day, she and her friend explored their newfound travel aid.

Join Amelia & her friends as they explore America's rich and powerful history! No adventure is off-topic as they meet some of our Nation's most influential figures from the Founding Fathers (and Mothers), to the greatest Freedom Fighters and lesser-known heroes.

Aimed at teaching children American history, this series does just that in a fun and colorful way that will appeal to all children!

Coming Soon- LilPatriotBooks.com

The All-American Curl Girl Beauty Pageant Coming Soon!

The All-American Curl Girl Beauty Pageant was founded for the curly-haired girls all over America struggling to see themselves as the All-American Girl. We want to create an environment where all beauty is created equal and traditional values are displayed to encourage curl power.

Our pageant is for girls of ALL races with naturally curly, wavy, kinky, and textured hair. Contestants will participate in the All-American Program leading up to the pageant. Winners will be rewarded with tuition to attend a local private school in their area, freeing them from their failing public schools.

Our Mission

For us to achieve our vision, we intend to ensure that we remain committed to:
- Serving our urban areas by building confidence in our young girls through our core values.
- Focusing on connecting with those with traditional values who share our philosophy.
- Partnering with those that are supporters of school choice.
- Building relationships with like-minded individuals, schools, businesses, and organizations to gain more continued support for our girls.

Our Vision

Our vision is to ensure that we are creating an environment where all beauty is created equal and traditional values such as classical feminism is displayed to encourage curl power.

Visit- AllAmericanCurlGirl.com
Facebook- All American Curl Beauty Pageant
Instagram- @AllAmericanCurlPageant

Robert Marshall

Robert Marshall is a lifelong Conservative since birth. Early in his life, he found the teachings of the Founding Fathers to be enticing and inspiring. His eyes lit up the first time learning about the history of our great Nation. The Declaration of Independence and The Constitution ignited a fire in his heart as he fell in love with the virtues of our founding.

Robert grew up in Prince George's County outside Washington, DC. Growing up in a lower-income area, he started to see the consequences of liberal policies that were plaguing the black community. Robert grew up in a family on welfare and experienced how government policies incentivized reliance on government aid and deterred self-reliance. From those early experiences in life, he turned to conservative values and principles as a solution to fix these issues and his community.

Throughout his teenage years, Robert knew that to transcend the station in life, he needed to focus on his education. In high school, he excelled in academics and was the first person in his family to be accepted and attend a university. While a freshman at Indiana University of Pennsylvania, the tragic event of 9/11 happened, and Robert was inspired to serve his country in the US Army proudly.

As a young, wide-eyed Soldier, he was deployed to Baghdad, Iraq in 2004, and served his country honorable. Upon returning from deployment, he still wanted to survive his country in a more impactful way and joined his university's ROTC program. Undergoing history and pre-law studies, he later became the first person in his family to achieve a college degree, and also the first person in his family to become a military officer.

In 2009, he was deployed to Iraq and became the leader of 50 infantrymen, successfully leading them into battle in Mosul, Iraq. His work with the local Iraqi police created a safer environment for the citizens of Mosul. He has been proud to serve his country in this capacity and honored that a man like him from the area of PG County could be a military officer.

After leaving the Army, Robert's mission has been championing conservative values and putting America first. He created a men's grooming business, Dapper Guru, where he is adamant in supporting the American economy by only sourcing American-made supplies and ingredients. He champions the idea that for African Americans to prosper in America, we need to focus on wealth building via small business ownership. He is heavily involved with the black conservative movement and is excited to see the growth of this movement and the energy behind it.

Dapper Guru: www.thedapperguru.com
LinkedIn: https://www.linkedin.com/in/robertmarshall1/
Twitter: @robertmarsl

Lisa Watson

Former liberal turned free-market education activist, Lisa Watson has a calling to disrupt failing schools. Read about her here:

In 7th grade, I received a letter from the Board of Education which opened the door for me to attend the #1 school in the state of Kansas. At only 13 years old, I couldn't understand how that letter would change the trajectory of my life.

The first person in my extended family to graduate college, I went on to earn my B.A. with a double-major in Psychology and Political Science.

Realizing at an early age that social advocacy was in my blood, I searched for ways to advocate for what I believed in. My college experience served to frame history through the lens of race and sex. That framework led me to a college internship with Planned Parenthood. My first job with a telecom company led me to a five-year stint as a Union Steward. Soon after, I was led to join the board of the Americans Civil Liberties Union; Positions include ACLU Affiliate Board member, Co-Chair of the ACLU Racial Justice Task Force,

ACLU Affirmative Action Officer, ACLU KC Chapter President, and ACLU National Board member in NYC. I was enjoying every minute of it. But fate had different plans for me. A divine appointment challenged me to re-think my world view and took my life in a radically new direction.

Newly dedicated to rising above unproductive partisanship, I have adopted Frederick Douglass' mantra, "I will unite with anybody to do right, and nobody to do wrong."

Understanding that, Black Lives won't Matter until Black Minds Matter, I now seek to educate Americans in general (Black Americans in particular), that access to quality K-12 education for every American student IS the civil-rights issue of the 21st century.

My social movement, "The Education Equality Revolution", seeks to replicate the exceptionally American successes of the Historically Black Colleges and Universities (HBCU's) by proving that, "If we can build colleges, we can build kindergartens.".

My patent-pending K-12 scholarship platform, "Citizenship Scholars" will serve to bridge the gap *between donors who appreciate President Reagan's warning that, "Freedom is never more than one generation away from extinction" and parents and schools who appreciate Malcolm Xs warning, "That only a fool would allow his enemy to educate his children."*

Visit- WatsonSpeaking.com
CitizenshipScholars.com

Black Conservative Federation

Black Conservative Federation

BCF Mission:
The Black Conservative Federation is a national network of GOP activists seeking to expand the Black conservative movement through a multi-pronged approach that addresses the disparities and apathy found in politically marginalized communities. Our integrity lies in disagreeing without being disagreeable, engaging without enraging, and demystifying conservatism in all communities.

BCF Vision:
Serving as the premier hub for Black conservatives throughout the country, the Black Conservative

Federation will provide the resources necessary for expanding and sustaining the conservative principles that work to strengthen and uplift our communities. Together, we will develop solutions for the most pressing issues facing both the black community and our country as a whole.

Who are we?
Our approach to expanding the movement consists of three tenets:

Economic Empowerment
- Promoting sufficient and reliable incomes, as well as dedication to credit building, budgeting, and access to financial literacy programs.

Excellence in Education
- The urgency of making meaningful connections becomes clear when we consider the dire consequences of students disengaging from school. Our approach to education encompasses school choice, college readiness, and vocational opportunities.

Community Engagement
- We believe in meeting people where they are. This means not just going into communities in search of a vote; We promote voter education, candidate advocacy and assistance, and grassroots involvement at all election levels.

Visit-BCFAction.com
Twitter- @BCFOfficial
Instagram- @BlackConservativeFederation

Diante Johnson

Diante Johnson is founder and president of the Black Conservative Federation (BCF). Under his leadership, BCF has evolved from a political networking group for black conservatives to an organization focused on political advocacy, outreach, and engagement. A native of Chicago and longtime resident of Danville, IL, Diante ran for his first political office at the age of 19. He also served on the then-presidential candidate, Dr. Ben Carson campaign.

He has both advised and worked on a number of state and local campaigns, most recently serving as North Carolina's Regional Field Director with the Donald J. Trump for President campaign. In October 2019 , Diante joined the 2020 Trump Campaign as a Black Voices for Trump Advisory Board member. In June of 2020, Diante was elected to represent Illinois as an At-Large Delegate at the 2020 Republican National Convention.

He was also elected to serve on the RNC 2020's Committee on Permanent Arrangements. Along with his multiple appearances on Fox News, CNN, OANN, Newsmax, and op-eds in the Washington Examiner and the Daily Caller, Diante has been recognized as Newsmax and Red Alert Politics' Most Influential "30 Under 30."

Twitter- @BCFPresident
Instagram- @Diante_Johnson

Book Services & Publishing completed by:

The WRITE Goals, LLC
7280 NW 87th Terrace
Suite C-210
Kansas City, Missouri 64153

www.thewritegoals.com
@thewritegoals

Made in the USA
Middletown, DE
08 April 2021